Modern American English

Robert J. Dixson
As Revised by Eugene J. Hall

5

New Edition

PRENTICE HALL REGENTS, Englewood Cliffs, New Jersey 07632

Library of Congress Cataloging-in-Publication Data

(Revised for vols. 3–5)
Dixson, Robert James.
Modern American English.
    Vol. 3–5 rev. by Eugene J. Hall
    1. English language—Textbooks for foreign speakers. 2. English
language—Grammar 1950– . 3. English language—United States.
I. Hall, Eugene J.
II. Title.
Pe1128.D515   1992   428.2'4   90–7104
ISBN 0–13–593914–3 (v. 1)
ISBN 0–13–593997–6 (v. 3)
ISBN 0–13–594060–5 (v. 4)
ISBN 0–13–594110–5 (v. 5)

Publisher: Tina B. Carver
Manager of product development: Mary Vaughn
Senior development editor: Nancy L. Leonhardt
Senior production editor: Tunde A. Dewey
Interior design and page layout: Function Through Form
Design supervision: Chris Wolf
Pre-press buyer: Ray Keating
Manufacturing buyer: Lori Bulwin
Cover design: Bruce Kenselaar
Cover photograph:©John Kelly/The Image Bank
Illustrations by Anna Veltfort

Published by Prentice Hall Regents
Prentice-Hall, Inc.
A Paramount Communications Company
Englewood Cliffs, New Jersey 07632

Printed in the United States of America

10 9 8 7 6

ISBN 0-13-594110-5

Prentice-Hall International (UK) Limited, *London*
Prentice-Hall of Australia Pty. Limited, *Sydney*
Prentice-Hall Canada Inc., *Toronto*
Prentice-Hall Hispanoamericana, S.A., *Mexico*
Prentice-Hall of India Private Limited, *New Delhi*
Prentice-Hall of Japan, Inc., *Tokyo*
Simon & Schuster Asia Pte. Ltd., *Singapore*
Editora Prentice-Hall do Brasil, Ltda., *Rio de Janeiro*

Contents

Preface

Modern American English 5 is the fifth of a series of six texts, with correlated workbooks and cassettes, designed as a complete course of study in English as a second language. The first two books provide elementary vocabulary and lay the foundations for a comprehension of the principles of English grammar; taken together, they can be considered to comprise a beginning course in English. The remaining books, the workbooks, and the cassettes build upon this foundation by expanding the study of vocabulary and completing the survey of English grammatical structures. Student book 6, although primarily a reader, provides a general review and additional practice on all the material previously studied.

The six books of the series have been planned for use in the junior high school, high school, or adult course of study. The pace of the books is measured but intensive, as is proper for students studying English on this level. Extensive oral practice is provided for everything presented. Students are prepared to move, without difficulty or confusion, from one step to the next, from one lesson to the following lesson. Vocabulary and grammar are controlled at all times, particularly at the beginning and intermediate levels in books 1 through 4. Consequently, there is no danger of teaching more vocabulary or structure than a student can readily absorb.

Expressed in a different way, the purpose of this book, as well as of the remaining books of the series, is to teach students how to use and understand spoken English. The approach emphasizes at all times the ability of the students to use what they have studied. All materials and all activities in the series contribute directly to this end.

Modern American English 5 is simple to use and easy to follow. It is a basic book consisting of fifteen lessons. Every fifth lesson is a review that provides additional practice on the material covered in the previous four lessons. Each of the remaining lessons is divided into four sections: *Reading and Oral Practice*; *Structure and Pattern Practice*; *Pronunciation and Intonation Practice*; and *General Practice*. Each of these sections is intended to give a particular kind of practice that will strengthen the students' learning experience and lead to their ability to communicate in the new language.

1. **Reading and Oral Practice.** This section introduces the material that is to be studied in the lesson. There are three parts to the *Reading and Oral Practice*. The first consists of a short narrative, arranged in paragraphs, each of which is followed by comprehension questions. The second part consists of questions and answers, cued to pictures, which give additional examples of vocabulary items, particularly idiomatic expressions, that are introduced in the lesson. The third part is a dialogue. All the new vocabulary in each lesson is presented in this section or in the grammar notes in the following section.

The first part of each section is intended primarily for listening and repeating practice and for comprehension. The students should first listen while the teacher reads each paragraph; then the students should repeat the paragraph after the teacher in chorus; next, individual students should be asked to repeat the paragraph; and finally, individual students should read the paragraph. After this preparation, the teacher should ask individual students to answer the comprehension questions that follow each paragraph. In addition to oral work in class, the teacher can assign the comprehension questions for written homework.

The next part of the section gives examples of vocabulary items and idiomatic expressions in the form of questions and answers that are cued to pictures. The teacher should use the same steps for introducing this material—choral repetition, individual repetition, and individual reading. The teacher should then use this material as a question and answer practice by asking individual students to give answers to the questions. Their books should be closed during this practice. As a final step, one student should ask the questions while another student gives the answers. This kind of student-student practice is highly recommended for all the exercises throughout the book.

Similar procedures should be followed for the dialogue, the third part of the *Reading and Oral Practice*. The steps should be listening, choral and individual repetition, teacher-student practice, and student-student practice.

2. Structure and Pattern Practice. This section is devoted to the study of grammatical structures and patterns in English. First, explanatory notes on the structure or structures are presented in the lesson. Each note is followed by one or more exercises to give the students practice on the pattern discussed in the preceding note. The exercises are intended to help the students achieve command of the formal features of English.

It is suggested that the teacher first go through each exercise orally, with students repeating each cue and its answer in chorus. In the next step, the teacher should present the cue and then ask the class to give the answer in chorus. After that, the teacher should give the cue, with individual students giving the answer. Wrong answers should be corrected immediately with the right ones, which the students should then repeat in chorus.

When sufficient oral work has been done, the teacher can assign the exercises as written homework. Homework should be corrected carefully and returned to the students so that they can note their errors and observe their progress. The exercises in this section are designed for habit formation on specific patterns, whereas the conversation practice in the final section of the lesson is designed to give the students greater flexibility in the *use* of the patterns.

3. Pronunciation and Intonation Practice. This section gives practice on different aspects of pronunciation. In this particular book, each lesson contains minimal pair drills on contrasted sounds. Many words are given in these drills that are *not* intended for vocabulary study, but *only* for pronunciation practice. For intonation practice, special exercises are marked with intonation patterns.

The material in this section should be presented by means of choral and individual repetition. The teacher's pronunciation and intonation will serve as a model for the students. The sentences for intonation practice should be said at a natural conversational speed so that the students will become accustomed to the sound of English as it is actually spoken. The cassettes give valuable additional practice for this section.

4. General Practice. This section gives oral practice on the actual use of English for conversational purposes. For those students who need or want to learn English so that they can genuinely communicate with other speakers of the language, this section is really the heart of the lesson.

All of the lessons include a controlled conversation practice. Questions are given which the students can answer from their own experience and knowledge within the structural and cultural framework of the patterns and vocabulary that have been studied. In this book, questions are given which provide opportunities for the students to state their opinions or to discuss their ideas. The teacher should encourage such discussion at all times. These questions are only suggestions. Each teacher should work out the particular questions which fit the reality of the particular situation and group of students.

SUPPLEMENTARY MATERIAL. A Teacher's Edition is available for each level of this series. For each book, a companion workbook is available in which each workbook lesson is closely coordinated with the corresponding lesson in its matching book. The workbooks provide additional material to help build all four of the language skills: listening, speaking, reading, and writing. For even more oral practice, cassettes may be obtained that cover the material in each of the book lessons.

Reading and Oral Practice

A. Listen and repeat. Then answer the questions.

Mrs. Harris had to call a repairman one day last week because her dishwasher had broken down. Down the street, the Rossis needed a repairman because their television was out of order. Another neighbor, Mr. Kramer, took his car to the garage the same day to get the brakes checked. By the end of the day, they had all spent a lot of money for repairs. Nowadays, homes and offices are filled with mechanical appliances and equipment, so maintenance and repair are a big part in the budget for most American families.

1. What did Mrs. Harris have to do one day last week?
2. Why did the Rossis need a repairman?
3. Why did Mr. Kramer take his car to the garage?
4. What had they all done by the end of the day?
5. What are homes and offices filled with nowadays?
6. What's a big part in the budget for most American families?

As a result, the repair business has grown very fast. It requires a lot of service people to keep all the equipment that we depend on in working condition. There are electricians and plumbers and automobile mechanics in every American town and city. Other service people take care of typewriters, air conditioners, or some other kind of machine. Some of them work for the companies that make or sell the equipment. Others have set up small businesses of their own.

7. What has happened to the repair business?
8. Why are a lot of service people required?
9. What is there in every American town and city?
10. What do other service people take care of?
11. What kind of companies do some of them work for?
12. What have other service people done?

There are many different ways in which these workers receive the necessary training. Some of them attend vocational high schools that specialize in technical skill training. There are also commercial vocational schools that offer courses in such subjects as air conditioning or television repair. Many other service people have worked for a while in a factory where one kind of machine is made. Others receive on-the-job training by working for someone who already has the technical skills. Electricians and some other repairmen are required to have a license in most parts of the United States.

13. Do all service workers receive their training in the same way?
14. What kind of schools do some of them attend?
15. What other kind of vocational school is there?
16. Where have many other service people worked?
17. What kind of training do others receive?
18. What are some repairmen required to have?

Repair jobs are considered to be blue-collar work. Blue-collar workers are employed in industry and construction. White-collar workers, on the other hand, are those who work in offices. In the past, white-collar workers were paid better than blue-collar workers. Nowadays, however, skilled blue-collar workers often make as much money as men and women who hold management jobs. The people who make the machines and keep them running play an essential part in today's technical world.

19. What are repair jobs considered to be?
20. Where are blue-collar workers employed?
21. Where do white-collar workers work?
22. Who was better paid in the past, white-collar or blue-collar workers?
23. Is this still the same?
24. How much money do skilled blue-collar workers often make?
25. Why do they make so much money?

B. Listen and repeat. Then answer the questions.

1. How do they know how much money they can spend?
   They have a budget that shows how much money they expect to get and to spend.

2. Why is there so much construction?
   The city keeps growing. As a result, more houses and buildings are necessary.

3. Does your repairman work for the store that sold you the appliance?
   No, he set up his own business. He set it up about a year ago.

4. Why hasn't she been attending a vocational school?
   She wanted to start working right away, so she's been getting on-the-job training from a plumber who has a lot of experience.

5. Why are office workers called white-collar workers?
   Because they used to wear white shirts to work.

6. Why are factory workers called blue-collar workers?
   Because they used to wear blue shirts to work.

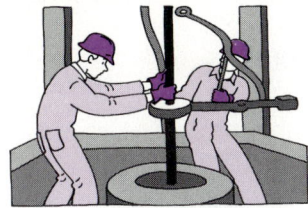

7. Why did they wear blue shirts?
   Because blue shirts don't show as much dirt as white shirts do.

8. Why are there so many vocational schools?
   They play an important part in training people in the technical skills that are essential in the modern world.

9. Why are you turning on the light?
   I'm turning it on because it's getting too dark to read.

10. Did you turn off all the lights?
    No, I didn't. I'll turn them off before I go to bed.

11. Why is the house so cold?
    The furnace went off, I don't know why. I've called the repairman.

12. Why is he looking for the flashlight?
    He's looking for it because the lights went out.

Thelma and Harry are relaxing at home in the evening.

THELMA: Please turn off that light, Harry!

HARRY: Why? What's the matter? I want to read the paper.

THELMA: If we turn on too many lights, all the electricity in the house will go off.

HARRY: Now who told you that?

THELMA: The electrician.

HARRY: The electrician? When was he here?

THELMA: I had to call him today.

HARRY: What was wrong?

THELMA: When I turned on the washing machine, all the lights went out.

HARRY: Well, didn't the electrician take care of it?

THELMA: Yes, but he said it would take a lot more work to do a really good job.

HARRY: What does he mean by a really good job?

THELMA: He said we needed new wiring all through the house and a lot of other things.

HARRY: Did he tell you how much it would cost?

THELMA: Yes, he gave me an estimate of about a thousand dollars.

HARRY: A thousand dollars! That's a lot of money. And just when we need to get some work done on the car too.

Structure and Pattern Practice

> *Have* or *has* plus *been* plus the *-ing* form of the main verb are used to form the present perfect continuous.
>
> I've been working hard all day.
>
> The present perfect continuous emphasizes the fact that an action begun in the past still continues in the present.
>
> He's been working on those repairs for a week (and he's still working on them).

A. Change to the present perfect continuous.

EXAMPLE

She's asked a lot of questions.   *She's been asking a lot of questions.*

1. He's gotten some on-the-job training.
2. They've trained a mechanic to fix all the machines in the office.
3. We've lived in the same apartment for two years.
4. They've built a lot of new houses in the suburbs.
5. She's written letters all day long.
6. You've considered the plan for a week.
7. I've chosen some new equipment for the office.
8. Their teacher has given them a lot of homework.

> The past perfect continuous is formed with *had* plus *been* plus the *-ing* form of the main verb.
>
> She had been expecting to get promoted.
>
> The past perfect continuous emphasizes that an action begun in the past continued up to the time of another past action.
>
> They had been having trouble with their car until they took it to a mechanic.

B. Change to the past perfect continuous.

He'd read the newspaper.   *He'd been reading the newspaper.*

1. He'd studied for a license as an electrician.
2. She'd specialized in chemistry.
3. I'd planned to become an architect.
4. Our company had done a lot of advertising.
5. The store had had a lot of sales.
6. We'd taken a course in air conditioning at a vocational school.
7. They'd spent a lot of money on maintenance.
8. The mechanic had worked on the car all day.

The question and negative forms are:

Have you been attending a vocational school?
I hadn't been looking for a car until I saw one
I really liked in a dealer's window.
Hasn't she been working in an office?

C. Change first to affirmative questions and then to negative questions.

He's been fixing the dishwasher.   *Has he been fixing the dishwasher?*
Hasn't he been fixing the dishwasher?

1. They've been holding meetings every week.
2. She'd been studying mathematics.
3. They've been making out their budget for next year.
4. They'd been spending too much money for maintenance and repair.
5. That school has been offering courses in vocational subjects.
6. You'd been renting an apartment before you found your house.
7. I've been driving to work every day this week.
8. They'd been saving a little money every month.

D. Change to the negative.

She'd been walking in the park.   *She hadn't been walking in the park.*

1. I've been resting and relaxing.
2. He'd been wearing a white shirt to work.
3. I'd been looking at new cars.
4. They've been taking care of all the appliances in their house.
5. She's been trying to learn some technical skills.
6. They'd been training some of their workers to make repairs.
7. We've been worrying about our budget.
8. They'd been giving the new employees on-the-job training.

Pronunciation and Intonation Practice

A. Repeat several times.

i as in *it*	*e* as in *ten*	*a* as in *at*
sit	set	sat
hid	head	had
bid	bed	bad
big	beg	bag
him	hem	ham
tin	ten	tan

B. Repeat these sentences.

1. He had a big hat on his head.
2. He had a big tan bag at the end of the rack.
3. I met him when he sat in back of me in class.
4. His back looked very big when he sat at his desk.
5. I have a stiff neck, a bad back, and an aching head.

ey king

EXAMPLE

She wants to do a really good job.

1. I had a really bad time.
2. It's a really important letter.
3. I had a really busy day.
4. He wore a really old coat.
5. They've bought a really expensive car.

General Practice

Conversation. Your teacher will ask you these questions or others like them. The questions will ask about things you can answer from your own knowledge or experience. You should give *real* answers to the questions.

What machines are most often used in homes in your country (or area)?

What machines are most often used in offices?

What kinds of repairmen are most needed in your city (or area)?

Would you like to be a repair worker? Why or why not?

How well are repair workers paid in your country (or area)?

How many vocational schools are there in your area?

What courses do the vocational schools offer?

Which do you think is more valuable for a repair worker, on-the-job training or classroom study?

Which are better paid in your country (or area), blue-collar or white-collar workers?

What are some kinds of blue-collar jobs?

Reading and Oral Practice

A. Listen and repeat. Then answer the questions.

An automobile is really a consumer product; that is, it is made for people to use directly; it is not used to make other products. A car, of course, is one of the biggest and most expensive of all consumer products. It is often said that a house and a car are the two largest purchases that people make in their lives. A car is a very complex piece of machinery. It consists of thousands of parts that must all work together. These parts are made in many different factories. The spark plugs, for example, may be made in one place and the carburetor in another. All these parts are finally brought to one place to be assembled into a car that will go out and join millions of others on the highways.

1. What kind of product is an automobile?
2. What is a consumer product?
3. Is a car a small product that doesn't cost much?
4. What are the largest purchases people make in their lives?
5. What kind of piece of machinery is a car?
6. What does it consist of?
7. Are all the parts made in the same place?
8. What automobile parts may be made in different places?
9. What happens to all these parts?

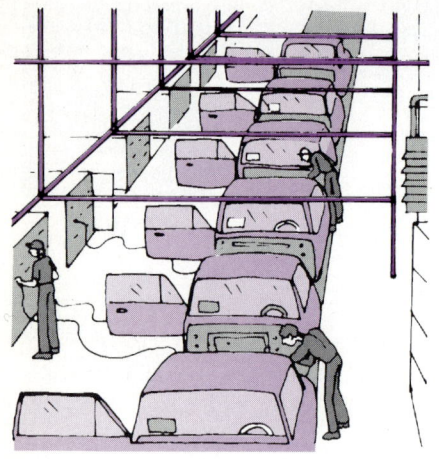

The factories where this work is done are called assembly plants. Each person on the assembly line usually works on only one part of the car. First the frame is put together. Then, as the car moves along the assembly line, other parts are added. After the cars are assembled, they are shipped to dealers all over the country.

10. Where are cars assembled?
11. What does each person on the assembly line usually work on?
12. What is put together first?
13. What happens next?
14. What happens to the cars after they are assembled?

The assembly line technique is called mass production. Through mass production, manufacturers can make large numbers of the same product quickly and cheaply. This usually means lower prices for consumers. Thousands of products from pencils to airplanes are made by mass production techniques. The high standard of living that many people enjoy today is in large part the result of the wide availability of products made on assembly lines.

15. What is the assembly line technique called?
16. What can manufacturers do through mass production?
17. What does this mean for consumers?
18. What is the result of the wide availability of products made on assembly lines?

Millions of blue-collar workers are employed in factories in the United States. Some of the factories are large; an automobile plant may cover hundreds of acres and employ thousands of people. Others are very small; many garment industry workshops in New York, for example, have only twenty or thirty workers. Several million factory workers in the United States belong to labor unions. The unions have helped many blue-collar workers to obtain wages as high as, or higher than, the salaries of white-collar workers. In addition, they have usually obtained health care and vacation benefits for their members.

19. Where are millions of blue-collar workers employed?
20. Are all factories large?
21. How large are some automobile plants?
22. What is an example of a small factory?
23. What do many factory workers in the United States belong to?
24. What have the unions generally helped them to obtain?
25. What else have they usually obtained for their members?

B. Listen and repeat. Then answer the questions.

1. What kind of job does he have?
   He has a service job; that is, he doesn't make anything; he provides people with a service.

2. Why did they call in the repairman?
   They have to fix a piece of machinery that broke down yesterday.

3. Where can I take my typewriter to be repaired?
   There's a shop across the street where you can take it to be repaired.

4. What does his work on the assembly line consist of?
   It consists of installing the carburetor.

5. Are you going to be taking your vacation in July again this year?
   No, I'm going to be taking it in the winter instead of the summer.

6. Why did she take so many math courses this year?
   She decided she wanted to be an engineer instead of an architect.

7. Are wages and salaries different?
   Yes, they are. Wages are figured by the hour, but salaries are figured by the week, month, or year.

8. How much per hour do the workers in that factory make?
   They make twelve dollars an hour.

9. How many vacation days a year will they be getting?
   They'll be getting twenty-one vacation days per year.

10. Why do a lot of people who work on assembly lines want to change jobs?
    They go on to different jobs because they get tired of doing just one task all the time.

11. Why didn't she put together her new stereo set herself?
    She didn't put it together because there were too many parts.

12. What's she looking for?
    She's looking for something new and different to wear.

Bill and Sandra work at a large assembly plant.

BILL:	Have you heard the good news?
SANDRA:	No, what is it?
BILL:	We'll be getting a raise soon.
SANDRA:	That *is* good news. When will it be starting?
BILL:	The middle of next month.
SANDRA:	How much more will we be getting?
BILL:	Twenty-five cents an hour.
SANDRA:	That's not bad, not bad at all. How did you hear about it?
BILL:	One of the union officials told me.
SANDRA:	Why haven't they announced it yet?
BILL:	They're still talking to management about some more benefits.
SANDRA:	What are they asking for?
BILL:	Extra vacation time, I think.
SANDRA:	That's fine, but when are they going to talk about making our work more interesting?
BILL:	That's a good question.
SANDRA:	I get tired of doing the same thing all day every day. I'd like to be doing something different sometimes. I may be looking for another job soon if they don't give me something new to do.

Structure and Pattern Practice

Continuous forms are also used with auxiliary verbs and idiomatic verb phrases. The auxiliary or verb phrase is followed by *be* and the *-ing* form of the main verb.

> I'll be talking to management next week.
> I'd better be leaving now.
> She'd rather be doing several different things instead of just one kind of work.
> It may be raining by the time we start home.

A. Change to the continuous.

EXAMPLE

You should take more math courses.
You should be taking more math courses.

1. She'll set up her own business in a few months.
2. They'll send us an estimate soon.
3. I'd rather watch a movie than television.
4. I may take a trip to California next month.
5. You'd better get ready for the exams next week.
6. You can put the addresses on the envelopes while I'm finishing the letters.
7. They're going to announce the raise soon.
8. They should talk to management about making the work more interesting.
9. They'll train us to use the computers next week.
10. He should send us the machinery soon.

In negatives, *not* also follows the first auxiliary.

> I may not be working here much longer if they
>   don't make the work more interesting.
> They aren't going to be getting any new
>   benefits this year.

B. Change to the negative.

EXAMPLE

He'll be writing programs for the computer.
He won't be writing programs for the computer.

1. You'll be operating the new machine.
2. The children should be watching television all the time.
3. He should be complaining about his job all the time.
4. They'll be giving us another raise next month.
5. She'll be studying math next year.
6. They'll be expecting us to arrive early.
7. The company should be doing more advertising.
8. She'll be calling you next week.
9. She'll be attending the rally tonight.
10. He'll be staying in the hospital for a long time

In questions, the subject follows the first auxiliary.

> Will we be getting that raise soon?
> Would you rather be working in an office or a
>   factory?
> Shouldn't you be doing your homework?

C. Change first to affirmative questions and then to negative questions.

EXAMPLE

She'll be writing programs for the computer.
Will she be writing programs for the computer?
Won't she be writing programs for the computer?

1. She should be waiting on this corner.
2. The plane will be arriving in the next few minutes.
3. They should be fixing the machines today.
4. They'll be constructing a new building here.
5. They should be training their new employees.
6. She'd rather be working in an office.
7. They'll be receiving more vacation time next year.
8. He should be making out his lesson plan for tomorrow.

Pronunciation and Intonation Practice

A. Repeat several times.

u as in *luck*	*o* as in *not*	*a* as in *cat*
cut	cot	cat
mud	mod	mad
luck	lock	lack
hug	hog	hag
cub	cob	cab
cup	cop	cap

B. Repeat these sentences.

1. You must have good luck to catch a cab.
2. He got mad when he got stuck in the mud.
3. The man was mad because I did not lock the door of the hut.
4. The cop did not break the lock at the back of the hut.
5. She got mad because I did not cut the grass at the back of the house.

C. Listen and repeat.

That is good news.

1. He is a high school graduate.
2. I am a repairman.
3. They are consumer products.
4. She was in class yesterday.
5. We were on time.

General Practice

Conversation. You should give *real* answers to these questions or others like them that your teacher will ask.

Do most of the people in your city (or region) depend on cars for transportation?

What other kinds of transportation are available in your city (or region)?

Are there many factories in your city (or region)? What do they make?

What things do you have that are made by mass production?

What things do you have that are *not* made by mass production?

Which do you prefer, things made in a factory or things made by hand? Why?

How big are most of the factories in your city (or area)?

What are the advantages of working in a large factory? What are the disadvantages?

What are the advantages and disadvantages of working in a small factory?

Would you like to work in a factory? Give your reasons.

Reading and Oral Practice

A. Listen and repeat. Then answer the questions.

"The business of America is business," President Calvin Coolidge once said. When you see one of the country's large cities, you can understand what he meant. In the center of the city, dozens of large office buildings contain banks, corporation headquarters, and government agencies. Every weekday morning, thousands of office workers enter these buildings, and then they leave for their homes every evening. Many of these people seem to be in motion all the time, in buses and taxicabs between one building and another, or in airplanes between one city and another.

1. What did Calvin Coolidge once say?
2. Where can you understand what he meant?
3. What is there in the center of large American cities?
4. What do thousands of workers do every weekday morning and evening?
5. What do many of these people seem to be?

The men and women who do all the office work are called white-collar workers. Secretaries and receptionists, bookkeepers and computer operators work for many different kinds of companies. There are big banks that do business all over the world and little banks that serve just one neighborhood or a small town. The big insurance and industrial companies employ thousands of people who work in huge skyscrapers, while around the corner an employment agency or a manufacturer's representative may have a staff of only half a dozen typists and bookkeepers.

6. What are people who do office work called?
7. What are some white-collar jobs?
8. Do all white-collar workers work for the same kind of company?
9. Where do big banks do business?
10. What do little banks serve?
11. What do the big insurance and industrial companies do?
12. Do all businesses have large staffs?

Many office workers dream of working their way up to the top, from messenger to president of the corporation. The way lies through middle management. Middle management includes junior executives, who may fill specialized jobs, supervise other workers, recommend action to top management, or see that the company's policies are being carried out. At the very top are the senior executives. They establish the policies for their companies, especially in financial matters. The top managers of the large corporations have a great deal of power and influence.

13. What do many office workers dream of doing?
14. How does a person rise to the top in a company?
15. What may junior executives do?
16. Who is at the very top?
17. What do the senior executives do?

It is still possible to start out at the bottom and go all the way to the top. Because financial matters are so important, some accountants become top executives. In companies where technology is important, people with an engineering background can also rise to the top. Nowadays, however, education plays a central part in the selection of men and women for management jobs. Many American universities offer courses in business administration. The graduates of these courses often start out in middle management jobs. From there, they can easily get promoted if they show the necessary personality and ability.

18. What is it still possible to do?
19. Why do some accountants become top executives?
20. What can happen in companies where technology is important?
21. What happens more frequently nowadays?
22. What do many American universities offer?
23. What happens to the graduates who have taken these courses?
24. What else do these graduates need to be promoted easily?

B. Listen and repeat. Then answer the questions.

1. Did her parents pay for her education?
   No, they didn't. She had to work her way through college.

2. What does he do when he gets tired?
   He lies down for a few minutes until he feels all right again.

3. How long has this report been lying around?
   It's been lying right there on your desk for a week.

4. Did she read the report right away?
   No, she didn't. It lay on her desk for a week before she even looked at it.

5. Why didn't he get a promotion?
   They feel he's lain down on the job. He just hasn't worked hard enough.

6. Do you think that young woman will be successful?
   I think she'll rise right to the top because of her personality and her ability.

7. How did she get to be a senior executive?
   She rose to the top because she knew so much about finance and accounting.

8. Has anyone ever risen to the top in this company?
   A few people have risen to top management jobs, but most of the jobs are filled by university graduates nowadays.

9. What kind of work can a computer carry out?
   It can carry out work with numbers and pieces of information.

10. Who sees that the workers carry out the company's policies?
    The junior executives usually see that the workers carry them out.

11. What kind of benefits will they get?
    For one thing, they'll get a small raise, and for another, they'll get more vacation time.

The irregular verbs *to lie* and *to rise* are introduced in this lesson.

    lie–lay–lain   rise–rose–risen

To lie is often followed by *down*.

    I was lying down when the phone rang.

C. Dialogue

Marcia and Phil are junior executives with a large computer corporation.

PHIL: What's going on around here? Why is everyone changing offices?

MARCIA: Haven't you heard? Where have you been anyway?

PHIL: I just got back from visiting the plant in Chicago.

MARCIA: Well, there are a lot of changes being made here this week.

PHIL: Yes, I see, but what are they?

MARCIA: For one thing, Marta and Jim are being transferred.

PHIL: Where are they going? Did they get promoted?

MARCIA: Marta's going to the office in Atlanta. She's going to be put in charge of the whole southern region.

PHIL: That sounds like a pretty good promotion to me. What about Jim?

MARCIA: He's going out to manage the plant in California.

PHIL: And you? What about you? Are you going to get transferred too?

MARCIA: No, I'm going to stay right here.

PHIL: Did you get promoted?

MARCIA: Not yet, but I'm hoping I will be.

PHIL: Don't you want to get transferred? I'd like that job in California.

MARCIA: No, I want to stay right here at the company headquarters. This is the place to get noticed by top management.

Structure and Pattern Practice

> Continuous forms also occur in the passive. A form of *to be* is followed by *being* plus the past participle of the main verb.
>
> > Several changes are being made in the office this month.
> > The policies were being carried out by the junior executives.

A. Change the verbs to continuous passive forms. Do not change the tense.

EXAMPLE

The lesson was taught by a new teacher.
The lesson was being taught by a new teacher.

1. The reports are written by a sales representative.
2. The house was designed by an architect.
3. The speech was given by a politician.
4. The new employees are trained by a supervisor with a lot of experience.
5. All the questions were answered by only a few students.
6. The necessary information is given by the computer.
7. Their wages are figured by the hour.
8. Her car was checked by a mechanic.
9. The budget was considered at the meeting.
10. The supplies are shipped by truck.
11. She was transferred to a branch office.
12. She's recommended by her supervisor.

> The question and negative forms are:
>
> Are all the jobs being filled by college
>   graduates nowadays?
> The work isn't being done fast enough.

B. Change to questions.

EXAMPLE

She's being assigned to a new job.   *Is she being assigned to a new job?*

1. The cars are being assembled in a huge new plant.
2. She is being required to take more math courses.
3. The students were being helped by their parents.
4. The machines are being fixed now.
5. Our company is being managed by a group of accountants.

C. Change to the negative.

EXAMPLE

She's being assigned to a new job.   *She isn't being assigned to a new job.*

1. The computer is being installed in another building.
2. The products are being sold in stores all over the country.
3. The package was being shipped by air.
4. The workers were being paid once a week.
5. The apartment is being rented by the month.

> A few common expressions can occur in the
> passive with *get* as well as with *be*.
>
> The package got lost in the mail.
> He'll get hurt if he isn't careful.
> I don't know how that machine got broken.

28

D. Change to the passive with *get*. Do not change the tense.

The machine was broken yesterday.   *The machine got broken yesterday.*

1. He was burned when he tried to put out the fire.
2. They were lost because they couldn't read a map.
3. They were assigned to a job they didn't like.
4. She was killed in an accident.
5. She'll be promoted next month.
6. He is bothered by a lot of little things.
7. The car will be fixed soon.
8. Several junior executives have been transferred this month.

Questions and negatives are formed in the same way as when *get* is a main verb.

Did he get hurt in the accident?
The letters didn't get sent out last night.

E. Change to questions.

The machine got broken yesterday.   *Did the machine get broken yesterday?*

1. The report got thrown away by accident.
2. The letters got sent out yesterday.
3. My friend got hurt in an accident.
4. She gets burned when she stays in the sun too long.
5. The candidate will get elected easily.

F. Change to the negative.

EXAMPLE

The machines get broken easily.   *The machines don't get broken easily.*

1. She gets assigned to all the easy jobs.
2. You'll get lost on the highway.
3. The packages will get shipped out this afternoon.
4. He got measured for a new suit.
5. We got sent to the meeting in Chicago.

Pronunciation and Intonation Practice

A. Repeat several times.

i as in *it*	*e* as in *eat*
it	eat
sit	seat
rid	read
hill	he'll
slip	sleep
is	ease
live	leave
tin	teen

B. Repeat these sentences.

1. I need to leave the place where I live at six on the dot.
2. If you sit in this seat, you'll be nearer the heat.
3. She'll eat it after you heat it.
4. He'll need to sit for a while before he gets to the top of the hill.
5. He'll see it if you leave it near the seat where he sits.

EXAMPLE

I'd like that job in California.

1. She took a course in business administration.
2. He'll get a top management job.
3. I can afford a new car.
4. He'll get noticed by management.
5. I can't recommend him for that job.

General Practice

Conversation.

What kinds of businesses are there in your city (or area)?

Would you rather work for a small business or a large one? Why?

What skills and experience are especially useful in the business world in your country (or region)?

In your country (or region) nowadays, is it easy or difficult for workers to work their way up?

What are some examples of large businesses? What are some typical small businesses?

Are there any universities in your country (or region) that offer courses in business administration?

What kind of education do you think is best for a career in business? What other kinds would be useful?

Reading and Oral Practice

A. Listen and repeat. Then answer the questions.

Ever since there have been towns and cities, there have been market centers. In some towns there were open-air markets where farmers could come and exchange their crops for cloth, pottery, and other articles that they needed. The temporary stalls that merchants set up soon became permanent stores where the merchants could show their merchandise all through the year. Most stores specialized in one kind of product, such as clothing or hardware. In many places the stores that sold the same products were close together on the same street or in the same corner of the market.

1. How long have towns and cities been market centers?
2. What were there in some towns?
3. What could farmers come there and do?
4. What happened to the temporary stalls?
5. What did most stores sell?
6. Which stores were located close together?

There are still millions of stores that specialize in only one kind of merchandise. Some stores sell only books or office supplies; some sell only men's or women's clothing; others sell only appliances or kitchen equipment. Nowadays, however, there are also department stores that carry everything that people need in the way of furniture, clothing, appliances, and dozens of other products. Department stores are convenient because shoppers can find all this merchandise under one roof. Supermarkets also provide one-stop shopping. People used to have to go first to the butcher, then to the baker, and so on, to buy all the food that they needed. Now they can get all kinds of food and supplies for the house at just one place. Another kind of market is the shopping mall where several stores that can take care of every need are located together. Shopping malls are a result of automobiles, so the most important feature of the typical mall is the parking lot that surrounds it.

7. Are there still stores that specialize?
8. What are some examples of specialized stores?
9. What other kind of store is there nowadays?
10. Why are department stores convenient?
11. What other kind of store provides one-stop shopping?
12. How did people shop for food before the supermarket?
13. What can they do now?
14. What is another kind of market?
15. What are shopping malls a result of?
16. What is the most important feature of the typical shopping mall?

All this activity of buying and selling is called merchandising. There are two different kinds of merchandising, wholesale and retail. The wholesale merchant buys products from manufacturers and sells them to the retail merchant, who then sells them to the public. There are thousands of products available today. The retail merchant would not be able to keep up with all of them without the services of the wholesale merchant.

17. What is the activity of buying and selling called?
18. Is there just one kind of merchandising?
19. What does the wholesale merchant do?
20. What does the retail merchant do?
21. Are only a few products available today?
22. Why is the wholesale merchant important to the retail merchant?

The consumer would not be able to keep up with all the products either without advertising. Advertising plays an essential part in modern merchandising. The manufacturers tell the public about their new products, and the stores tell the public what products are available at what prices. There are advertisements in newspapers, magazines, and on television every day of the week. In addition, many more advertisements are mailed directly to customers. Careful shoppers watch the ads to find bargains when sales are announced. This huge business of merchandising employs millions of white-collar workers, from clerks in the stores to top executives in the big department stores and advertising agencies. For most clerks the salaries are low, but salaries for top executives are among the highest in the United States.

23. How does advertising help the consumer?
24. Is advertising important in modern merchandising?
25. What do manufacturers tell the public?
26. What do stores tell the public?
27. Where and when are there advertisements?
28. How do many more advertisements go to customers?
29. What do careful shoppers do?
30. Are many people employed in merchandising?
31. Are all the salaries in merchandising high?

B. Listen and repeat. Then answer the questions.

1. Who are all these new people in the office?
   They've hired several temporary employees because the work has been heavy. They'll only be here for two or three weeks.

Come work for us.

2. How did she get her job?
   She started out as a temporary employee, but her work was so good that they gave her a permanent job.

3. Why are there so many shopping malls nowadays?
   There are a lot of shopping malls because there are so many automobiles.

Office Supplies

4. What does that store sell?
   It sells everything in the way of office supplies from pencils to office furniture.

35

5. Do they have different buildings for the elementary school and the high school?
   No, they don't. They're both under one roof.

6. Where do you take your car for service?
   I take it to a garage that really gives one-stop service. They do everything from selling gasoline to making major repairs.

7. Why does she always have so much information about what's going on?
   She keeps up with everything by reading newspapers, magazines, and books all the time.

8. Why didn't they finish all the work today?
   They got started on it too late to finish all of it today.

9. Do you want to look at this report now?
   No, not now. Put it aside, and I'll look at it tomorrow.

10. Why did that sales representative get a promotion?
    She brings in a lot of business that makes money for the company. She brings more in than the other representatives.

Jeanne and Eduardo work in the advertising department of a big
department store.

JEANNE: What have you got there?

EDUARDO: Requests for advertising space from the different departments.

JEANNE: There must be a couple of dozen of them!

EDUARDO: Yes, every department in the store must be having a sale this week.

JEANNE: How much space do we have available?

EDUARDO: We've only got enough to meet half of these requests.

JEANNE: Then we're going to have to make some decisions.

EDUARDO: Yes, we certainly are. I suppose we should go through all of them.

JEANNE: Yes, we should. Shall we get started?

EDUARDO: Well, this one on top is from the children's department. But their
sale doesn't begin until next week.

JEANNE: Then you can put it aside. What's the next one?

EDUARDO: From furniture, and their sale starts tomorrow. They've got some
really good bargains too.

JEANNE: What about the women's departments?

EDUARDO: There are half a dozen of them—women's dresses, young women's
sports clothes, coats, shoes—

JEANNE: Those departments all bring in a lot of business, you know.

EDUARDO: Then let's give them the most space in tomorrow's ads. A full page
for the women's departments and a half page for furniture.

Structure and Pattern Practice

> *Have got/has got*, usually in contracted form, is a frequent substitute for *to have* as a verb of possession.
>
> > They have a new car.
> > They've got a new car.
> >
> > She has a new dishwasher in her kitchen.
> > She's got a new dishwasher in her kitchen.
>
> *Have got/has got* is used in the present tense. It does not commonly occur in the past.
>
> *Have got/has got* is also used conversationally for *must* or to *have to*.
>
> > You must send these letters out today.
> > You have to send these letters out today.
> > You've got to send these letters out today.
>
> In this usage, *have got/has got* has present or future significance.

A. Change *must, has, have,* or *have to* to *have got/has got.*

EXAMPLE

We have air conditioning in our office.
We've got air conditioning in our office.

1. I have a sewing machine that can do anything.
2. You must take a bus to get to the city.
3. They have to find a way to make the job more interesting.
4. They have some good bargains in the store this week.
5. You have to keep up with all the news.
6. The sales representatives must bring in more business.
7. He has two telephones on his desk.
8. You have to get started on this job right away.

Shall is an auxiliary verb which is generally used only with questions in the first person—*I* or *we*. *Shall* asks for advice or agreement with a proposed action.

> Shall we send this package out by air?
> Shall I do these letters next?

B. Change the form of *to be going to* to *shall*. Note that the meanings of the sentences will not be the same after the change.

EXAMPLE

Are we going to watch television tonight?
Shall we watch television tonight?

1. What am I going to do if my car breaks down?
2. What are we going to do if they don't bring in more business?
3. Are we going to get started on the report this afternoon?
4. When are we going to visit your family?
5. Are we going to have a sale in the women's departments?
6. Are we going to give the new employees on-the-job training?

The auxiliary verbs often have special meanings in addition to their principal ones.

Won't is often used in the sense of *refuse*.

> She refuses to help me with my work.
> She won't help me with my work.

C. Change these sentences so that they use *won't* instead of *refuse*.

She refuses to write any letters for me.   *She won't write any letters for me.*

1. He refuses to answer any questions.
2. The boss refuses to recommend me for a promotion.
3. They refuse to transfer him.
4. They refuse to install air conditioning in the office.
5. They refuse to give the workers any more benefits.
6. He refuses to worry about his health.

Must is used to indicate probability as well as necessity.

Advertising is probably very important to their business.
Advertising must be very important to their business.

Must have is a past form of must. It is used only in the sense of probability.

They look happy. They must have had a
good time on their vacation.

D. Change these sentences so that they use must or must have instead of probably.

She's probably at lunch now.   *She must be at lunch now.*

1. They probably sold their old car.
2. The bus probably stops at this corner.
3. Her secretary probably writes all her letters.
4. He probably heard the weather report on the radio.
5. They probably get all their groceries at the supermarket.
6. They probably saw the advertisement for the sale.
7. They probably keep up with everything by reading the newspaper.
8. She probably repaired the car herself.

> *Mustn't* is used to indicate an action that is forbidden or not allowed.
>
> > You aren't allowed to talk in the library.
> > You mustn't talk in the library.

E. Change these sentences so that they use *mustn't* instead of *not allowed*.

EXAMPLE

You're not allowed to eat in the museum.   *You mustn't eat in the museum.*

1. The children aren't allowed to watch television every evening.
2. They aren't allowed to build houses in the park.
3. You aren't allowed to walk on the grass.
4. You aren't allowed to talk in class.
5. We aren't allowed to ask any questions.
6. You aren't allowed to walk in the street.

Pronunciation and Intonation Practice

A. Repeat several times.

e as in *me*	*a* as in *may*	*i* as in *lie*
me	may	my
meet	mate	might
read	raid	ride
leak	lake	like
seen	sane	sign
team	tame	time
meal	mail	mile

1. He might make you a meal if you say please.
2. I've seen no sign that we're near the right place.
3. He'll see if he can get the mail here on time.
4. She'll say that it's time to make another meal.
5. We'll all leave the place at the same time.

C. Listen and repeat.

EXAMPLE

I love that color!

1. I love your new scarf!
2. I love eating in French restaurants!
3. He loves rich food!
4. The children just love milk!
5. She loves math and science!

General Practice

Conversation.

Is your city (or town) well known for one special kind of product?

What kinds of specialized stores are there in your town (or neighborhood)?

Do you prefer to shop in small, specialized stores or in department stores and supermarkets? Why?

Are there many shopping malls in your area? How many stores are there in them?

Do you like to shop in a mall? Why?

What kind of advertising do you see? What kind do you really look at?

Would you like a job in merchandising? Why?

What should you do to be a careful shopper?

Structure and Pattern Practice

A. Change to the corresponding continuous form.

EXAMPLE

They've made some changes in the factory.
They've been making some changes in the factory.

1. The top management jobs were filled by junior executives.
2. They had required all their employees to take on-the-job training.
3. We will ship your order next week.
4. The union has asked for new benefits for the workers.
5. She was recommended for a promotion.
6. The new workers are supervised by someone with a lot of experience.
7. They should have a sale in the women's departments.
8. They must keep up with all the most recent news.
9. I'd rather work in an office than a factory.
10. Our advertising is taken care of by a large agency.
11. That sales representative has brought in a lot of new business.
12. They had worked under dangerous conditions.
13. The executives will talk about financial problems at the meeting.
14. The conditions in the factory are improved every week.
15. He should make out his lesson plans.
16. She'll have a good time all summer.

They've been making some changes in the factory.
Have they been making some changes in the factory?

 1. The old machines are being replaced.
 2. He's been receiving a lot of letters recently.
 3. She had been reading all the best sellers.
 4. She'll be representing the people of her district in Congress.
 5. He had been speaking to the voters.
 6. All the information is being provided by the computer.
 7. She should be teaching mathematics.
 8. They are being trained in a vocational high school.
 9. I've been keeping up with all the news. (you)
10. They should be announcing the raises soon.

C. Change to the negative.

They've been making some changes in the factory.
They haven't been making any changes in the factory.

 1. We had been collecting unemployment pay.
 2. She'll be running for Congress next year.
 3. We were being followed down the street.
 4. They'll be using the computer for all their accounting work.
 5. You should be drawing unemployment pay.
 6. The machines are being operated by that new employee.
 7. He's been having trouble with his science classes.
 8. She'll be getting a pension next year.
 9. We should be leaving early.
10. They'll be moving to Florida soon.

D. Change to the passive with *get*.

When was he assigned to his new job?
When did he get assigned to his new job?

1. Her schedule was approved without any trouble.
2. A lot of people are married in the spring.
3. He wasn't noticed by the top executives.
4. She's going to be promoted next month.
5. How was your typewriter broken?
6. He wasn't elected to Congress.
7. Won't we be lost if we don't have a map?
8. She's sent out of town on a lot of business trips.
9. Nobody was killed in the accident.
10. I was fired last month.

E. Change these sentences so that they use *have got/has got*.

She has a business of her own.
She's got a business of her own.

1. I must get my typewriter fixed soon.
2. You have to turn off all the lights before you go upstairs.
3. They have a lot of new employees in the office.
4. She has a license as an electrician.
5. They have to give the workers a raise.
6. The union must try to get more benefits from management.
7. You have to change the spark plugs.
8. The president of the company has a lot of power and influence.
9. They must do more maintenance on those machines.
10. You have to call a repairman.

F. Change these sentences so that they use *won't* instead of *refuse*.

They refuse to exchange the merchandise.
They won't exchange the merchandise.

1. Management refuses to give us extra vacation time.
2. They refuse to ship our supplies by air.
3. We refuse to join a union.
4. The boss refuses to recommend me for a middle management position.
5. They refuse to train the new employees.
6. The children refuse to go outside on cold days.
7. They refuse to give us enough technical training.
8. I refuse to work for a large corporation.
9. He refuses to give us an estimate.
10. She refuses to recommend me for a raise.

G. Change these sentences so that they use *must* or *must have* instead of *probably*.

They probably obtained a raise for the workers in the factory.
They must have obtained a raise for the workers in the factory.

1. They probably do a lot of maintenance and repair work.
2. She probably ordered the office supplies.
3. They're probably high school graduates.
4. They probably turned off the air conditioning.
5. Her car probably broke down.
6. She probably owns her own business.
7. They probably need new wiring all through the house.
8. She probably attended a vocational high school.
9. He probably missed the bus this morning.
10. She probably saw the ad for the sale in this morning's newspaper.

EXAMPLE

You aren't allowed to talk in the library.
You mustn't talk in the library.

1. We aren't allowed to use the new machines.
2. We aren't allowed to turn on the lights.
3. You aren't allowed to sleep here.
4. You aren't allowed to eat at your desk.
5. He isn't allowed to talk to the other employees.
6. The aren't allowed to go to the movies before they finish their homework.
7. She isn't allowed to operate the computer.
8. They aren't allowed to work overtime.
9. You aren't allowed to fix the machines yourself.
10. They aren't allowed to change the budget.

I. Change *to be going to* to *shall*. Note that the meaning will be changed.

EXAMPLE

Are we going to attend the meeting this afternoon?
Shall we attend the meeting this afternoon?

1. Are we going to buy a new refrigerator?
2. Am I going to talk to the new employees?
3. Are we going to show the merchandise in the store window?
4. Am I going to use the computer for this job?
5. Are we going to throw away these old magazines?
6. Am I going to meet you after work tonight?
7. Are we going to stay home tonight?
8. Am I going to join a health club?
9. Are we going to consider the budget at the meeting tomorrow?
10. Am I going to have lunch with my friends today.

General Practice

A. Reading comprehension. Read the paragraph and then answer the questions.

Mark Kozlowski was born and brought up in a small industrial city in the Middle West. The most important factory in town was an automobile assembly plant. Mark's father and uncle both work on the assembly line. Mark expected to go to work there himself when he finished high school. It seemed like an easy life with good pay, a life he would share with all his friends. His father, however, had very different ideas. He told Mark that he should go on to the university and get a degree in engineering. For one thing, he warned Mark, he couldn't always be sure of work in the factory. A lot of automobiles are manufactured when times are good, but when times are bad, a lot of workers lose their jobs. Mark's father believed that Mark would have more security in management than in a blue-collar job. Mark listened to his father and accepted what he said. Now he is finishing his last year in high school, taking a lot of math, and keeping his grades high.

1. Where was Mark Kozlowski born and brought up?
2. What was the most important factory in town?
3. Who works on the assembly line?
4. When did Mark expect to go to work there?
5. What kind of life did it seem to him to be?
6. What did his father have?
7. What did he tell Mark?
8. What did he warn Mark?
9. What happens when times are good?
10. What happens when times are bad?
11. What did Mark's father believe?
12. What did Mark do?
13. What is he doing now?

B. Conversation.

What are some examples of blue-collar jobs?

What are some examples of white-collar jobs?

Which are better paid in your country (or area), blue-collar or white-collar jobs?

Which kind of work would you prefer, blue-collar or white-collar? Why?

What kinds of machine do you know how to use?

Are there many factories in your city (or region)? What do they make?

What kinds of transportation are available in your city (or area)?

Do you think transportation in your area could be improved? How?

What kinds of office jobs are available in your city (or region)?

What kind of education do you think is best for a business career? Why?

Would you like a job in advertising or merchandising? Why?

Would you rather shop in large stores or small ones? Why?

Do you think you are a careful shopper? What do you do to be careful?

Reading and Oral Practice

A. Listen and repeat. Then answer the questions.

For a long time the Crawfords have been saving money toward buying a house in the suburbs. Last week they finally found a house that they both loved, so they've signed a contract to buy it. They'll make a down payment and then get a mortgage to cover the rest of the cost. They shouldn't have any trouble getting a mortgage because they both have jobs. Most people need to borrow money in order to buy a house. It costs a lot, though, because they have to pay interest on their loan for many years.

1. What have the Crawfords been doing for a long time?
2. What did they find last week?
3. What have they signed?
4. What will they make?
5. How will they cover the rest of the cost?
6. Why shouldn't they have any trouble getting a mortgage?
7. What do most people need to do in order to buy a house?
8. Why does a mortgage cost a lot?

Banks pay interest on most checking and savings accounts. They charge a higher interest, however, on the money they lend, and that's how they make a profit. For example, Sylvia Ortiz has a savings account that pays 5 percent interest. Last year she bought a new car and borrowed money from her bank for most of the cost. She will have to pay 8 1/2 percent interest on her loan for five years. Of course she has to pay only $150 a month, so it doesn't seem like quite so much money when the cost is spread out.

9. On what do banks pay interest?
10. How do they make a profit?
11. What does Sylvia Ortiz have?
12. What did she do last year?
13. How much interest will she have to pay and for how long?
14. How much does she have to pay a month?
15. Why won't that seem like quite so much money?

Credit is easy to get in the United States for people who have jobs or a regular income. Millions of people have credit cards that are issued by banks. Ted Costas got a credit card after he'd been working for a few months. He went to the mall the next day and saw a lot of things he'd always wanted to buy. With his card it seemed terribly easy to buy them all. All he had to do was give the salesclerk his card; he didn't need to take any cash out of his wallet or write a check. It's a year later now, and Ted is still paying for his shopping spree. It will take him a long time to pay off all the money he owes because the interest charged on credit card debts is very high.

16. Who can get easy credit in the United States?
17. What do millions of people have?
18. When did Ted Costas get a credit card?
19. What did he do the next day? What did he see?
20. Why did it seem terribly easy to buy everything?
21. What is Ted still doing a year later?
22. Why will it take him a long time to pay off the money he owes?

There are a lot of other kinds of credit. Gasoline companies, for example, issue credit cards so it isn't necessary to pay cash for gas and oil or routine service. Department stores have charge accounts to make it easier to buy their merchandise. Most stores that sell expensive items – appliances and furniture, for example – offer credit of one kind or another. It always seems so easy until the time comes to pay, and then the purchaser finds that it's necessary to pay not only the price of the item but also a large amount in interest.

23. What do gasoline companies issue?
24. What do department stores have?
25. What other kind of stores offer credit?
26. What does the purchaser find when the time comes to pay for something?

The irregular verb *to spread* is introduced in this lesson.

    spread–spread–spread

Spread is often followed by *out*.

    I spread out all the packages on the table.

B. Listen and repeat. Then answer the questions.

1. When did they make the down payment on their house?
   They made the down payment when they signed the contract.

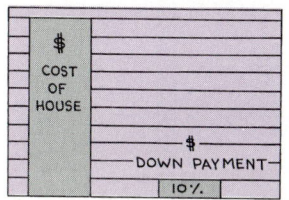

2. What percent of the total cost was the down payment?
   The down payment was 10 percent of the cost.

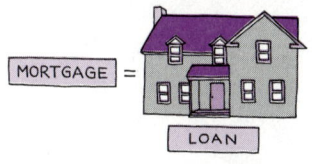

3. What is a mortgage?
   A mortgage is a special kind of loan for a house or other property.

4. How long will it take them to pay off their mortgage?
   It will take them twenty years to pay it off.

5. How long will she spread out the payments on her car?
   She'll spread them out for five years.

6. Will the bank lend her money for a new car?
   They'll lend it to her if she has a job.

C. Dialogue

Roger has just opened a checking account and is having trouble balancing his first statement.

ROGER:	I can't make this come out right.
SARAH:	What are you trying to do?
ROGER:	I got my bank statement today, so I'm trying to balance my account.
SARAH:	That should be easy.
ROGER:	It doesn't seem to be easy for me. I don't understand how to do it.
SARAH:	You add all the checks that haven't cleared through the bank. Then you subtract that total from the amount the bank shows.
ROGER:	Should that be equal to what I show in my checkbook?
SARAH:	Yes, if you haven't made a mistake in adding or subtracting.
ROGER:	Check it for me, will you?
SARAH:	Okay. Are these all checks that haven't cleared yet?
ROGER:	Yes, all of them.
SARAH:	You've got quite a lot of them.
ROGER:	I paid all my bills last week. How much money do I have left?
SARAH:	A hundred twenty-four dollars and seventy-nine cents. Is that what your checkbook shows?
ROGER:	Yes, exactly. I was hoping I'd made a mistake. I'm going to have to take some money out of my savings account to get through the month.

Structure and Pattern Practice

The present participle—the -ing form of the verb—is used after all prepositions except to.

> He's responsible for establishing policies.
> They've talked about installing a computer to do all the accounting work.
> Banks depend on lending out money to make a profit.

Some verbs are followed by the present participle rather than by an infinitive. Some of them are enjoy, finish, and understand.

> I haven't finished writing the report yet.
> We enjoyed watching the football game.
> It's stopped raining.

Note that when to stop is followed by an infinitive, it is an infinitive of purpose.

> He stopped using his credit card. (He doesn't use his credit card anymore.)
> They stopped to get gasoline. (They stopped for the purpose of getting gasoline.)

The -ing form can also be used as the subject of a sentence.

> Eating the right kind of food is important for your health.
> Installing the computer isn't going to be an easy job.

A. Complete with the present participle of the verb in parentheses.

EXAMPLE

He enjoys ⎯⎯⎯⎯⎯ (work) with the computer.
He enjoys working with the computer.

1. They've started ⎯⎯⎯⎯⎯ (ship) their products by truck.
2. We're thinking about ⎯⎯⎯⎯⎯ (move) to the suburbs.
3. ⎯⎯⎯⎯⎯ (live) in the suburbs will be a big change for us.
4. ⎯⎯⎯⎯⎯ (eat) in a restaurant every day is very expensive.
5. You'll have to try ⎯⎯⎯⎯⎯ (find) this information for me.

6. He's afraid of _____ (drive) in traffic.
7. She's responsible for _____ (operate) all the machines in the office.
8. They talked about _____ (put) their money in a savings bank.
9. _____ (try) out the programs is necessary before you operate the machines.
10. He hasn't finished _____ (balance) his checkbook.
11. They decided on _____ (establish) an office in Atlanta.
12. They're buying property instead of _____ (sell) it.
13. _____ (have) all this information will help management a great deal.
14. They finished _____ (give) their new employees on-the-job training.
15. She's depending on _____ (get) a loan from the bank.

B. Complete with both the present participle of the verb in parentheses and the appropriate preposition.

I'm afraid _____ (ride) my bike in city traffic.
I'm afraid of riding my bike in city traffic.

1. He's responsible _____ (provide) management with all the information that they need.
2. She never worries _____ (make) mistakes.
3. He's adding those checks to his account instead _____ (subtract) them.
4. They get tired _____ (do) the same task all the time on the assembly line.
5. They're talking _____ (give) the workers more benefits.
6. He's in charge _____ (write) programs for the computer.
7. We're not sure _____ (find) workers with the right kind of technical training.
8. That machine is used _____ (check) the brakes.
9. I'm interested _____ (learn) to use a computer.
10. He's afraid _____ (set) up his own business.

A few verbs can be followed by either the present participle or the infinitive. They include *begin, like, love, prefer, try,* and *start.*

It's started to rain. I tried to balance my account.

It's started raining. I tried balancing my account.

C. Change the infinitive to a present participle.

He prefers to work in the computer section.
He prefers working in the computer section.

1. The typists don't like to use the new machines.
2. They began to operate the computer before the programs were ready.
3. They prefer to fill the jobs with workers who have experience.
4. She started to work on the report at nine o'clock.
5. They prefer to live in the city.
6. He should try to balance his checkbook.
7. It hasn't begun to rain yet.
8. You have to try to learn how to use a computer.
9. She loves to answer all the questions.
10. They've started to give all the new employees on-the-job training.

Pronunciation and Intonation Practice

A. Repeat several times.

o as in *not*	*ou* as in *bought*	*oa* as in *coat*
not	naught	note
cot	caught	coat
tot	taught	tote
rot	wrought	wrote
sod	sawed	sewed
cod	cawed	code
fond	fawned	phoned

B. Repeat these sentences.

1. He taught the tot everything that he knows.
2. The boat that she bought has not yet gotten out to sea.
3. She had not taught me that I ought to stay still in the boat.
4. She brought me a note that he wrote but not one that she wrote.
5. She could not get the cod that she caught into the boat.

C. Listen and repeat.

EXAMPLE

I felt so hungry!

1. That store is so expensive!
2. The movie was so exciting!
3. That mistake was so bad!
4. I'm so full!
5. She's always so busy!

General Practice

Conversation.

Do you rent the place where you live or do you own it?

How expensive are houses in your neighborhood or area?

If you have a mortgage, how much interest are you paying?

Have you ever borrowed money from a bank? What for? How much interest did you pay?

Do you have any credit cards? What do you use them for?

Have you ever had to pay off a credit card debt? How much interest did you have to pay?

Do you have a bank account? What kind is it? How much interest does it pay?

What kind of bills do you have to pay every month? How do you pay them?

Do you think it's too easy to get credit in the United States? Give your reasons.

Reading and Oral Practice

A. Listen and repeat. Then answer the questions.

Modern transportation, communications, advertising, and credit have all combined to create a giant new industry called tourism. Tourism is a service industry. It doesn't make a product that people can own; instead it provides services on a temporary basis. The customer receives a seat on an airplane, a room in a hotel, and a chance to sit on a beach in the sunshine. The customer may be traveling for pleasure, for business, or for many other reasons. Whatever the reason, the traveler needs a way to travel and places to sleep and eat. To take care of these needs, tourism has created millions of jobs in hotels, restaurants, and transportation companies. Many of these jobs provide experience for people who have never worked before.

1. What things have combined to create a giant new industry?
2. What is this industry called?
3. Why is tourism considered a service industry?
4. What does the customer receive?
5. Why may a customer be traveling?
6. What does a traveler need?
7. What has tourism created to meet these needs?
8. What do many jobs in tourism provide?

Until modern times, a trip was often a long and difficult adventure. Traveling by horse or camel or on foot was slow and frequently painful. The roads were usually bad—unpaved and often dangerous. Places to stay frequently provided nothing more than a roof over one's head. Travel by water was generally a little easier, but ships were slow and they had to try to avoid storms at sea.

9. What was a trip like until modern times?
10. How was traveling by horse or camel or on foot?
11. How were the roads?
12. What did places to stay provide?
13. What other way of travel was generally a little easier?
14. What problems were there with ships?

The first development in modern transportation was the steamship, which could sail against the wind. Then came the railroads. They carried large numbers of people quickly over long distances for low fares. More recently, automobiles and airplanes have made travel both faster and more convenient. A trip across the ocean that would have taken weeks only a hundred years ago now takes just a few hours. As it became easier to travel, better places to stay sprang up. At first hotels were built near railroad stations in big cities. Then seaside areas that were served by railroads became the first popular resorts. Since the time of automobiles and airplanes, more and more areas have become resorts. Hotels have sprung up along tropical beaches or in mountain areas where people can get away from crowded cities.

15. What was the first development in modern transportation?
16. What could the steamship do?
17. What was the next development in transportation?
18. What did the railroads do?
19. How have automobiles and airplanes changed travel?
20. How have trips across the ocean changed?
21. Where were hotels built at first?
22. What became the first popular resorts?
23. Why have more and more areas become resorts?
24. Where have hotels sprung up?

Advertising has played a large part in the growth of tourism. Hotels and governments began to advertise the attractions of different tourist areas, and then transportation companies advertised the low fares necessary to reach them. Modern communications were put to work so that travelers could make reservations right away for a plane seat or a hotel room. And they could travel now and pay later by using their credit cards. All of these have combined to create the constant movement that has become one of the features of modern life.

25. What has played a large part in the growth of tourism?
26. What did hotels and governments begin to do?
27. What did transportation companies do then?
28. How were communications put to work?
29. How could travelers travel now and pay later?
30. What have all of these things combined to create?

B. Listen and repeat. Then answer the questions.

1. Why does he live downtown?
   He likes to be able to go everywhere on foot.

2. What does that hotel provide?
   It can take care of all one's needs—a place to sleep, food, even shops.

3. Are they building many new houses in your area?
   Yes, new houses spring up all the time. There seems to be another new one every day.

4. What made the suburbs grow so fast?
   They sprang up because cars made it easy for people to move out of the cities.

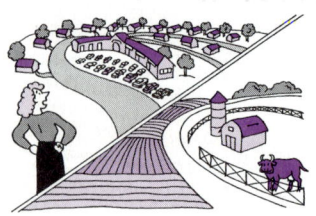

5. I don't remember these houses and shopping malls. They've sprung up in no time at all. This was a farm two years ago.

6. Where is the hotel?
   It's right beside the beach.

7. Where's the garage?
   It's next to the house. It's right beside the kitchen door.

8. Why don't you want to stay at that hotel?
   I don't like the food. Besides, there isn't enough to do there.

9. Why aren't you going to travel by plane?
   It's too expensive. Besides, I'm afraid of flying.

10. Why are they moving to the suburbs?
    They want to get away from the dirt and noise of the city.

The irregular verb *to spring* (*up*) is introduced in this lesson.

   spring–sprang–sprung

Also note the difference between *beside* and *besides*. *Beside* means *next to*, while *besides* means *in addition (to)* or *anyway*.

Also note the use of *one* as an impersonal pronoun, similar in meaning to the impersonal *you*.

   You can get everything you need in a department store.
   One can get everything one needs in a department store.

MRS. BARRY:	What part of the paper are you reading?
MR. BARRY:	The travel section.
MRS. BARRY:	Are you thinking about our vacation already?
MR. BARRY:	Yes, it's not so far away. I've been looking at some of these ads for cruises.
MRS. BARRY:	Why don't we just go to the same place we went last year?
MR. BARRY:	I won't stay at that hotel again. There wasn't enough to do.
MRS. BARRY:	Do you have a better idea for this year?
MR. BARRY:	Yes, I do. Look at this ad. This looks like a wonderful vacation to me.
MRS. BARRY:	"Three weeks." "Ten exciting ports." "Use the ship as your hotel." How much does it cost?
MR. BARRY:	We'd have to call a travel agent to get the price.
MRS. BARRY:	It must be expensive if they don't give the price in the ad. And besides, I'd rather just stay in one place.
MR. BARRY:	I don't want to sit on the same beach and eat the same food and look at the same walls every day for three or four weeks.
MRS. BARRY:	You know the doctor said that you shouldn't try to do too much.
MR. BARRY:	He didn't say that I had to sit in the same chair all day long.
MRS. BARRY:	Well then, call the travel agent and find out how much the cruise costs.
MR. BARRY:	Let me have the paper back, and I'll do it right now. And I'll get some information on other cruises too.

Structure and Pattern Practice

A few common adjectives are followed by the infinitive. Many sentences with these adjectives begin with *it is*.

It's easy to spend too much money when you use your credit cards all the time.
It's difficult to fix the machines.

Other common adjectives that are used in sentences of this kind are *hard, important, possible, necessary,* and *interesting*.

It's necessary to provide training for all the new employees.
It isn't possible to stay within the budget.

A prepositional phrase with *for* is used to give the subject when it is necessary to state it.

It isn't possible for me to stay within the budget.
It's necessary for you to order supplies this week.

A. Change these sentences so that an infinitive follows the adjective.

E X A M P L E

Advertising all the sales isn't possible.
It isn't possible to advertise all the sales.

1. Trying out the new programs is necessary.
2. Shippping this order by air is important.
3. Working on an assembly line isn't very interesting.
4. Living in the city is convenient for them.
5. Operating the new machines isn't difficult.
6. Finding workers with technical experience is hard.
7. Living in a big city like New York is exciting.
8. Carrying out the policies of management is necessary.
9. Saving money isn't easy.
10. Looking at the camels was interesting.

B. Add the prepositional phrase with *for* in the correct place.

It's necessary to solve this problem. (for the students)
It's necessary for the students to solve this problem.

1. It's difficult to balance my checkbook. (for me)
2. It hasn't been easy to settle down. (for him)
3. It isn't possible to break down. (for this machine)
4. It's important to have all the information they can get.
   (for management)
5. It's necessary to provide them with the information. (for us)
6. It wasn't easy to get the workers another raise. (for the union)
7. It was easy to train the new typists. (for the supervisor)
8. It was hard to set up my own business. (for me)

The infinitive is also used to show purpose. In this case it answers the question *why*.

> Why did she call a repairman? To fix her dishwasher.
> She called a repairman to fix her dishwasher.

The infinitive of purpose is sometimes preceded by the expression *in order to*.

> He called a meeting in order to consider the budget.

The infinitive after *stop* is always the infinitive of purpose.

> He stopped talking to me. (He stopped the action of talking.)
> He stopped to talk to me. (He stopped for the purpose of talking.)

C. Combine the questions and answers into sentences using the infinitive of purpose.

Why did he stop? He wanted to ask me a question.
He stopped to ask me a question.

1. Why does she attend night school? She wants to study business administration.
2. Why did he call his travel agent? He wanted to get prices on some cruises that he'd seen advertised.
3. Why did you go to the cafeteria? I wanted to get a cup of coffee.
4. Why did they try out the new programs? They wanted to make sure that there were no mistakes in them.
5. Why did they install the computer? They wanted to provide management with more information.
6. Why has she opened a savings account? She wants to save some money.
7. Why did he quit his job? He wanted to find more interesting work.
8. Why did he look at the ads in the paper? He wanted to find some bargains.

Pronunciation and Intonation Practice

A. Repeat several times.

o as in *not*	*ou* as in *bought*	*ow* as in *now*
bot	bought	bout
tot	taught	tout
rot	wrought	rout
cod	cawed	cowed
fond	fawned	found
pond	pawned	pound

B. Repeat these sentences.

1. The dog pawed at the lawn before she found her bone.
2. She taught the tot not to talk too loud.
3. He had bought about a pound of cod.
4. The hound that he'd bought fawned on him.
5. She had wrought a beautiful pot out of the clay that we found on the edge of the pond.

C. Listen and repeat.

EXAMPLE

What a busy day I had!

1. What a wonderful person she is!
2. What a hard job he has!
3. What an expensive coat he bought!
4. What a difficult problem that was!
5. What a nice letter she wrote me!

General Practice

Conversation.

What kinds of transportation serve your city or area?
Is there much tourism in your country or area? What are the attractions?
What kinds of jobs does tourism provide?
Would you like a job in tourism? Give your reasons.
What is the best trip you ever had? Why did you like it?
What is the worst trip you ever had? Why was it so bad?
What are some of the places you would like to visit? Why?
Do you think it's a good idea to travel now and pay later? Give your reasons.

Reading and Oral Practice

A. Listen and repeat. Then answer the questions.

Last week Tim Chung found a ticket on his car when he got out of work. He'd parked in a place where it was illegal to leave his car after five o'clock. The same day Marta Pintero received a notice that her income tax payment was overdue. On that same day, the sanitation crew picked up the trash at the Kleins' house, and the letter carrier delivered Mrs. Bradley a long letter from her daughter. All of these people had come in contact with government in one way or another on that day.

1. What did Tim Chung find last week?
2. Where had he parked?
3. What did Marta Pintero receive the same day?
4. What happened at the Kleins' house on that same day?
5. What did the letter carrier deliver to Mrs. Bradley?
6. What had all these people come in contact with?

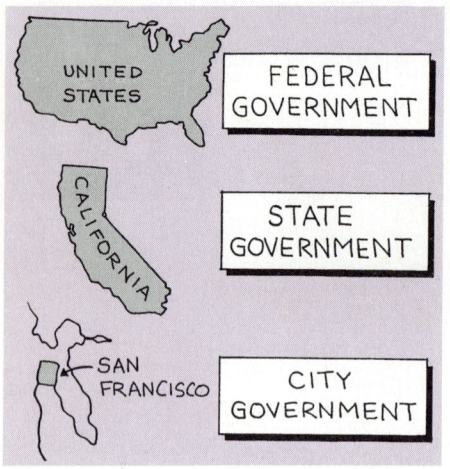

Government is a big business in the United States today. In fact, there are lots of different levels of government. There are local governments in cities and towns, counties, and the fifty states that make up the nation. At the top is the federal government, which makes and administers laws for the whole country. Tim Chung's ticket was issued by his local police force, and the Kleins' trash was collected by another local government agency, the sanitation department. Marta Pintero's notice, on the other hand, came from the Internal Revenue Service, an agency of the federal government. And Mrs. Bradley's letter was delivered by the Postal Service, another federal agency.

7. Is government a big or a small business?
8. Is there only one level of government?
9. Where are there local governments?
10. What is at the top? What does it do?
11. Who issued Tim Chung's ticket?
12. Who collected the Kleins' trash?
13. Where did Marta Pintero's notice come from?
14. Who delivered Mrs. Bradley's letter?

Local governments have the most direct influence on our lives. For one thing, they regulate our existence with the automobile by building roads, issuing licenses, and deciding where we can park. Local governments are also responsible for education, from kindergarten through high school or even beyond, in state universities and community colleges. Think of all those millions of school teachers throughout the country, all of them government employees! So are police officers, fire fighters, librarians, ambulance crews, and many others. Money to operate city and county governments comes largely from property taxes. Most of the state governments collect income taxes and also charge a tax on sales.

15. What do local governments seem to have?
16. How do they regulate our existence with the automobile?
17. What else are local governments responsible for?
18. Do they provide education beyond high school?
19. What is a large group of government employees?
20. Who are some other government employees?
21. Where does the money to operate city and county governments come from?
22. What do most of the states do?

WHITE HOUSE   SENATE   CONGRESS

SUPREME COURT

The president and the vice president, the members of Congress and the Supreme Court, are the superstars of the federal government. They're the ones who get all the headlines and whose faces we see on television every day. There are millions of other people, however, who work for the federal government. For example, there are all the men and women in the army, navy, and air force. There are also thousands of office workers, "bureaucrats" as they are often called. They handle all the paperwork in the hundreds of bureaus, agencies, and departments that make up the federal government.

23. Who are the superstars of the federal government?
24. What do they get?
25. Where do we see their faces?
26. Are there any other people who work for the federal government?
27. What is an example?
28. Who else is there?
29. What are these people often called?
30. What do they do?

1. When are you going to pick up those packages?
   I'm going to pick them up tomorrow.

2. Do you have much contact with the federal government?
   No, not much. In fact, the only time I come in contact with it is when I send in my income tax payment.

3. Are you going home for the holidays?
   Yes, I'll get there one way or another.

4. Do you have a lot of work today?
   Yes, there was lots of mail this morning.

5. Did you receive a lot of letters today?
   I didn't receive many letters, but I did get lots of bills.

6. Is your office the only one in the department?
   No, it's only one of about a dozen that make up the department.

7. Are those government jobs any good?
   They don't pay as well as jobs in private industry.
   On the other hand, they offer lots of security.

8. Why is he having such a hard time getting a job?
   Because he never went beyond high school.

9. Where is the post office?
   It's down the street, just beyond the museum.

10. Why is she filling out all those forms?
    She's filling them out so she can get a
    government job.

11. When are you going to fill out your income
    tax return?
    I'm going to fill it out next week.

12. Why is he looking for a job?
    He got fired from the one he had last month.

Lots of is an alternate form for *a lot of*. It is followed by a mass noun or a plural count noun, exactly like *a lot of*.

MARTIN: What are you doing?

ROSA: I'm filling out an application.

MARTIN: An application for what?

ROSA: For a government job.

MARTIN: The city government?

ROSA: No, the federal government.

MARTIN: You don't want to be another one of those bureaucrats, do you?

ROSA: I sure do.

MARTIN: Oh, government jobs aren't any good.

ROSA: Yes, they are. For one thing, they pay pretty well.

MARTIN: Not as well as jobs in private industry.

ROSA: But I want security. It isn't easy to get fired from a government job.

MARTIN: If you get the job, you'll have to spend your whole life in some boring office.

ROSA: Not my whole life. I'll be able to retire after thirty years, and I'll get a good pension.

MARTIN: Thirty years is a long, long time.

ROSA: I can take early retirement after twenty years and still get a pension.

MARTIN: Twenty years. Well, that's not too bad.

ROSA: Here, I have another application. You can take it and fill it out.

Structure and Pattern Practice

> Adjectives in English have only one form for both the singular and the plural.
>
> new car–new cars; big factory–big factories

A. Change to the plural.

> EXAMPLE

Her new dress is in the closet.   *Her new dresses are in the closet.*

1. There's a big store in the neighborhood.
2. It's a large building.
3. The old car is in the garage.
4. There's a new employee in the computer section.
5. That's a beautiful house.
6. This is a useful product.
7. She's a careful worker.
8. It's a complex machine.

> Descriptive adjectives (*large, small, new, expensive*) come before the noun that they describe.
>
> He's thinking about buying a small car.
>
> Intensifiers (*too, very, really*) come before the adjective that they intensify (make stronger).
>
> They took a very expensive cruise last year.
> She was wearing a really beautiful dress.
>
> Adjectives of nationality (*Peruvian, Japanese, French*) come after descriptive adjectives. Note that the adjectives of nationality always begin with a capital letter in English.
>
> She liked the small Japanese car that she saw last week.

Noun adjuncts are nouns that are used as adjectives. They are almost always singular with the exception of *sports,* which usually occurs in the plural form. They come directly before the noun to which they refer.

> She likes that red Italian sports car.
> They make expensive winter coats in that workshop.

Prepositional phrases and clauses modifying nouns come after the noun to which they refer.

> Many of the clothing factories in New York are quite small.
> They make stereos in the *factory that we visited last week.*

B. Add the word or expression in parentheses in its correct place.

EXAMPLE

The store sells appliances. (on the corner)
The store on the corner sells appliances.

1. They had dinner in a small restaurant. (Italian)
2. She's writing some important letters. (very)
3. I finally bought a small car. (Japanese)
4. He's wearing a sweater today. (green)
5. The suit didn't cost much. (that he bought)
6. The people want small ones. (who buy cars today)
7. I'm reading a book. (interesting)
8. There's a big table in the classroom. (steel)
9. She wore a long skirt to the party. (silk)
10. We want to get a car. (red)
11. The products are sold to the general public. (that are made in this factory)
12. That factory doesn't make products. (consumer)
13. All the parts are made in different plants. (of a car)
14. They're installing a complex system. (computer)
15. I've found a good plumber. (really)
16. She got her training on the job. (technical)

Pronunciation and Intonation Practice

A. Repeat several times.

u as in *put*	*oo* as in *school*
full	fool
pull	pool
stood	stewed
hood	who'd
would	wooed
soot	suit

B. Repeat these sentences.

1. She stood and looked while I stewed the fruit.
2. Who'd like to show me the book that has all the rules of the school?
3. If he could have wooed her, he would have.
4. You'll have to look at the new book of rules.
5. Take a good look at the tools that you should learn how to use.

C. Listen and repeat.

EXAMPLE

How hungry I am!

1. How tired I feel!
2. How exciting this story is!
3. How beautiful they looked!
4. How shy he is!
5. How hard this job is!

General Practice

What different levels of government are there in your country (or area)?
Who is in charge of education in your country (or area)?
Who is in charge of the police in your country (or area)?
What contacts have you had with government in the last year?
What taxes do you have to pay?
What are some kinds of government jobs in your country (or area)?
Would you like to have a government job? Give your reasons.

Reading and Oral Practice

A. Listen and repeat. Then answer the questions.

You pay your taxes, but everything still seems to be a mess. There are so many cars on the road that it takes you longer and longer to get to work every day. And over there, where there used to be a big field, they're building more houses, and that will mean more people, more cars, and more pollution. And speaking of pollution, the air was so bad yesterday that it was hard to breathe. What's the government doing about all these things, you may ask yourself, when you're paying all these taxes? Probably you'll just shrug and tell yourself that there isn't anything you can do.

1. How does everything seem even though you pay your taxes?
2. Why does it take you longer to get to work every day?
3. Where are they building more houses?
4. What will the new houses mean?
5. How was the air yesterday?
6. What may you ask yourself?
7. What will you probably do?

But you *can* make government listen to you—it's your government, after all. The people who work for it call themselves public servants, and you are part of the public. The government officials who set policies will certainly pay attention to the way you vote. Their jobs depend on your vote. If they win the next election, they'll keep their jobs, but if they lose, they'll be out of work. Your one vote may not seem important, but many elections are decided by only a handful of votes. This is especially true in local elections, but it sometimes happens even in national elections for the president and vice president.

8. Why can you make government listen to you?
9. What do the people who work for government call themselves?
10. What will government officials pay attention to?
11. What do their jobs depend on?
12. What will happen to them as the result of the next election?
13. Why may your one vote be important?
14. When is this especially true?
15. Does it ever happen in national elections?

Local governments usually respond to public pressure much more quickly than the state and federal governments. There are a lot of ways to put pressure on local governments. Most of them hold public hearings about almost every action they are called on to take. It's a lot easier to go to meetings in your own town than to go to Washington or the state capital. And if you can get together with some of your neighbors who share your opinions, it makes your voice even stronger. A group can often get publicity for its ideas in the newspapers or on television. A group can also ask for help from the courts to make the government obey the law.

16. What level of government responds to public pressure more quickly?
17. Is there only one way to put pressure on local governments?
18. What do most of them hold?
19. Where is it easiest to go to a meeting?
20. What can make your voice even stronger?
21. What can a group often get?
22. What else can a group do?

Groups are especially important in trying to influence the federal government. The big labor unions, for example, have Washington offices with men and women who try to persuade members of Congress to vote one way or another. And the labor unions are not alone. There are hundreds of other organizations that work at influencing the policies of the federal government. They are expert at manipulating public opinion to gain support for their own ideas. When you see pictures of a demonstration in Washington, you can be sure that someone has organized it. And you can also be sure that someone knows where the camera is so the pictures will get on the TV evening news.

23. In what way are groups especially important?
24. What do the big labor unions have?
25. What do hundred of other organizations do?
26. What are they expert at?
27. What can you be sure of when you see pictures of a demonstration in Washington?
28. What else can you be sure of?

1. Was she unhappy when they assigned her to the training program?
   No, not at all. After all, it was her own idea.

2. Why are all those people going to the hearing?
   They want to make the government pay attention to their opinions.

3. Why doesn't he do well in school?
   He pays less attention to the teacher than he should.

4. Did a lot of people attend the meeting?
   No, only a handful. There were fewer than ten people there.

5. Why are they having a public hearing tonight?
   They've been called on to put some more money in the budget for highway improvements.

6. Do they have regular meetings?
   No, they get together only when they want to discuss a special problem.

7. Have they been able to get people to pay attention to their ideas?
   No, they haven't. They've received less publicity than they expected.

8. What are you planning to go into?
   I can't decide whether to go into business or government.

9. What are you planning to do for a career?
   To start with, I'm going to get an engineering degree. Then I'm going into industry.

10. When did you begin to map out your career?
    I mapped it out while I was still in high school.

11. Why does he want to get a new job?
    He wants to find one that's less boring than the one he has now.

12. Did he make a big success of his career in politics?
    No, he didn't. He was much less successful than he thought he'd be.

C. Dialogue

Paul has just graduated from law school. His friend Tina attended the graduation.

TINA: What are you going to do now that you have your law degree?

PAUL: I'm going into politics.

TINA: You sound very sure of yourself.

PAUL: I am. I studied law so I could go into politics. After all, law is the business of government.

TINA: Aren't you going to set up your own practice?

PAUL: I've been offered a position in a law firm, but I want to get started on my political career right away.

TINA: What office are you going to run for?

PAUL: The state legislature, to start with.

TINA: To start with? Have you got your career all mapped out already?

PAUL: Yes, I have. After I've had some experience at the state level, I'll run for Congress.

TINA: Don't you want to try to run for governor of the state?

PAUL: No, I want to go to Washington. The state governments have much less power nowadays than the federal government.

TINA: I didn't know you were so ambitious.

PAUL: I'm interested in public service. Who knows, perhaps after a few years in Congress, I might even have the chance to run for president!

TINA: You're forgetting the great danger in politics, aren't you? You can lose elections as well as win them.

PAUL: If that ever happened, I'd still have my law degree, you know.

Structure and Pattern Practice

In addition to positive comparison of adjectives—
smaller and *the smallest,* for example, or *more
important* and *the most important*—there are
negative comparisons that use *less* and the *least.*

> That job was less difficult than I expected.
> That's the least interesting book that I've read
>   this year.

Less is also used with adverbs.

> I've seen her less frequently than I used to.

A. Change these sentences so that they use a negative comparison
with *less*.

He isn't as ambitious as he sounds.
He's less ambitious than he sounds.

   1. The weather isn't as windy as they said it would be.
   2. My new chair isn't as comfortable as I thought it would be.
   3. He isn't as interested in his job as he used to be.
   4. The problem isn't as serious as they thought.
   5. You won't get there as quickly by train as by plane.
   6. She isn't as happy as I expected her to be.
   7. This report isn't as important as he said it was.
   8. The computer isn't as useful as we expected.
   9. The information wasn't as useful as it should have been.
  10. The work wasn't carried out as quickly as we had planned.

B. Change these sentences so that they use *the least* instead of *the most*.

She sat in the most comfortable chair in the room.
She sat in the least comfortable chair in the room.

1. She has the most important job in the office.
2. They're having the exams at the most convenient time possible.
3. That's the most pleasant news that I've ever heard.
4. It was the most exciting experience that we ever had.
5. That's the most useful course you can take.
6. That's the most beautiful tie that he's ever worn.
7. This is the most interesting report that I've ever received.
8. It's the most useful machine we have in the office.

With nouns, *less* is used with mass nouns.

> They should use less electricity than they do.
> We've received less information than we need.

Fewer is used with plural count nouns.

> There aren't as many cars on the streets on
>   Saturday and Sunday as during the week.
> There are fewer cars on the streets on Saturday
>   and Sunday than during the week.

> They haven't been hiring as many new
>   employees this year as they did last year.
> They've been hiring fewer new employees this
>   year than last.

The negative superlative forms, *the least* and *the fewest*, are not often used with nouns.

C. Complete with *less* or *fewer*.

She makes _____ mistakes than I do.
She makes fewer mistakes than I do.

1. Local governments have _____ power than the federal government.
2. I seem to have _____ time every day to finish my work.
3. We have _____ electrical appliances in our house than our neighbors do.
4. They give their new employees _____ technical training than they should.
5. Our candidate got _____ votes than we expected.
6. Management always seems to have _____ information than necessary.
7. We get _____ help from the government than we need.
8. They're doing _____ advertising this year than last.
9. We've had _____ requests for our new products than the sales department expected.
10. I keep _____ money in my savings account than I should.
11. There has been _____ growth in industry this year than there should have been.
12. I write _____ checks than my wife does.
13. There are _____ roads in our neighborhood than we need.
14. They're making _____ improvements in the highway system than they should.
15. I have _____ income than I'd like to have.

Pronunciation and Intonation Practice

A. Repeat several times.

oy as in *boy*	*i* as in *time*
boy	buy
toy	tie
soy	sigh
loin	line
foil	file
toil	tile

B. Repeat these sentences.

1. I have to buy some toys for my boy.
2. These coins won't buy many toys for my boy.
3. I wish the boy would try only one toy at a time.
4. I've been foiled in every try I've made to find those files.
5. The boy doesn't know how to tie his own tie.

C. Listen and repeat.

EXAMPLE

You'll have to call a travel agent.

1. She wants to get a sports car.
2. You have to watch the traffic light.
3. Tourism is a service industry.
4. He works in the computer section.
5. She got a job with a law firm.

General Practice

Conversation.

What officials do you vote for in local elections?

What officials do you vote for in national elections?

When did you last vote? Do most of the people in your country or region usually vote?

Do you think people should vote in every election? Give your reasons.

What are some of the problems that you think your local government should pay attention to?

What are some of the policies that you think your national government should either continue or change?

Have you ever joined a group that was trying to influence the government? Tell about it.

Would you like to have a career in politics? Give your reasons.

What do you think government can do to help you or to make your life better?

Structure and Pattern Practice

A. Complete these sentences with both the present participle of the verb in parentheses and the appropriate preposition.

I'm afraid _____ (break) my leg if I go skiing.
I'm afraid of breaking my leg if I go skiing.

1. The job consists _____ (put) the carburetors in cars.
2. She's responsible _____ (supervise) the new employees.
3. I depend _____ (get) a statement from my bank every month.
4. They've been talking _____ (balance) the budget.
5. He dreams _____ (become) president.
6. I get tired _____ (do) the same kind of work all the time.
7. She's interested _____ (find) a more exciting job.
8. This machine is used _____ (make) keys.
9. He should get a job instead _____ (hang) around the park all day.
10. He's in charge _____ (issue) licenses.
11. They're thinking _____ (close) the store early.
12. He has to take care _____ (order) the new supplies.
13. He's going to keep _____ (study) math.
14. She can't get a promotion in spite _____ (be) a good worker.

B. Change the infinitive to a present participle.

He prefers to work in the computer section.
He prefers working in the computer section.

1. They tried to fix the brakes in my car.
2. They tried to organize a big demonstration.
3. The company prefers to hire people with a technical background.
4. She'll begin to study mathematics next year.
5. He started to map out his career while he was still very young.
6. She loves to supervise the new employees.
7. I'd prefer to leave in the morning.
8. Do you like to keep up with all the latest news?
9. They'll begin to work on the budget next week.
10. He prefers to stay on in Los Angeles.

C. Change these sentences so that an infinitive follows the adjective.

Advertising all the sales isn't possible.
It isn't possible to advertise all the sales.

1. Getting publicity for their opinions is difficult.
2. Firing a government employee isn't easy.
3. Deciding on a career while you're still in school is important.
4. Running for political office is exciting.
5. Understanding financial problems is necessary for top management.
6. Seeing a lot of different countries is interesting.
7. Becoming a doctor is hard.
8. Creating a lot of new jobs through tourism is possible.
9. Getting a license is necessary.
10. Learning to use a computer is easy.

D. Combine the questions and answers into sentences using the infinitive of purpose.

Why did he stop? He wanted to ask me a question.
He stopped to ask me a question.

1. Why is she taking the exam? She wants to get a government job.
2. Why are they giving the exam? They're trying to fill some positions in the government.
3. Why is he writing all those letters? He wants to find a new job.
4. Why is she balancing her checkbook? She'd like to find out if she made a mistake.
5. Why are they buying all that space in the newspapers? They want to advertise all their January sales.
6. Why is she taking her car to the garage? She wants to get the spark plugs replaced.
7. Why are the officials of the union talking to management? They want to obtain more benefits for the workers.
8. Why did he join a political club? He wanted to run for public office.
9. Why did she get to school early? She wanted to talk to her professor.
10. Why did they buy bicycles? They were trying to get more exercise.
11. Why does she go to night school? She wants to learn computer programming.
12. Why is she going to the grocery store? She wants to buy some bread and milk.
13. Why are the children hurrying? They want to get to school on time.
14. Why is she checking all the letters? She wants to find any mistakes in them.
15. Why are they having a meeting? They want to consider the budget.
16. Why does she read the newspaper every day? She wants to keep up with the news.

EXAMPLE

The police officer will help you. (on duty)
The police officer on duty will help you.

1. They've planned some interesting activities. (really)
2. When did she get her degree? (law)
3. He wears an old shirt at work. (blue)
4. The people don't want to give the workers a raise. (who own the factory)
5. She's an ambitious young woman. (very)
6. They're out riding around in their new car. (Japanese)
7. Men and women are difficult to fire. (with government jobs)
8. The government is issuing more money. (paper)
9. Management always needs more information. (useful)
10. The advertisement will appear in tomorrow's paper. (for the sale)
11. She brought back some beautiful pottery from her trip. (Italian)
12. She checks her statement every month. (bank)
13. There will be a management meeting tomorrow. (important)
14. She's going to wear her new dress to the party. (red)
15. The city government has a good pension plan. (very)
16. He has a new shirt. (cotton)
17. She's been reading a bestseller. (interesting)
18. She was trying on a new dress. (summer)
19. The cafeteria isn't very expensive. (in our building)
20. The boy is my brother. (who's sitting over there)

F. Change these sentences so that they use a negative comparison with *less*.

EXAMPLE

He isn't as ambitious as he sounds.
He's less ambitious than he sounds.

1. The desk wasn't as expensive as the chair.
2. His work isn't as careful as we'd like it to be.
3. It isn't as windy today as it was yesterday.
4. Factory work isn't as dangerous as it used to be.
5. The exam wasn't as difficult as she'd heard.
6. He isn't as famous as he thinks he is.
7. Train service isn't as frequent as it was a few years ago.
8. She doesn't write to her parents as often as they'd like.

G. Complete with *less* or *fewer*.

EXAMPLE

She makes _____ mistakes than I do.
She makes fewer mistakes than I do.

1. The city has _____ employees than it needs.
2. I found _____ bargains in the stores than I'd expected.
3. There's _____ construction in the city than in the suburbs.
4. The union has _____ members than it used to.
5. There's _____ industrial than commercial development in the community.
6. I always have _____ cash than I need.
7. They've received _____ benefits than they asked for.
8. We need _____ laws, not more.
9. They've gotten _____ publicity than they expected.
10. There's _____ unemployment now than there was a year ago.

General Practice

A. Reading comprehension. Read this paragraph and then answer
the questions.

   Kay Sheppard heard that a big new office building was going to be
constructed near her house. She lives in a neighborhood of comfortable homes
on small pieces of property. There are a couple of shopping streets with small
stores in the area. Most of the families have children because there's an
elementary school nearby. Kay wasn't happy when she heard about the new
building. She felt that it would change the whole neighborhood. There would
be more people and more traffic. The streets would be more dangerous for the
children on their way to school. When she talked to her neighbors, she found
that they weren't happy either. She and two or three other women began to
organize a group to stop the project. Now almost everybody in the
neighborhood has joined the group. They've gotten publicity by telling their
story to the local newspapers and TV stations. Next week they're going to a
public hearing to put pressure on the city government.

1. What did Kay Sheppard hear?
2. What kind of neighborhood does she live in?
3. Where do people shop in the area?
4. Why do most of the families have children?
5. Why wasn't Kay happy when she heard about the new building?
6. What would there be?
7. How would the streets be?
8. What did she find when she talked to her neighbors?
9. What did she and some other women do?
10. How many people have joined the group now?
11. How have they gotten publicity?
12. Where are they going next week? Why?

B. Conversation.

Would you like to work in a bank? Why?

Would you like to work in a hotel or restaurant? Why?

Would you like to work in a government agency? Why?

Do you think it's a good idea to buy things on credit? What kind of things? Give your reasons.

Do you think tourism is a good business for a country or region? Give your reasons.

Do you think there's too much government or too little? Give your reasons.

Do you think it's possible to change the policies and actions of government? How can it be done? Give your reasons.

Reading and Oral Practice

A. Listen and repeat. Then answer the questions.

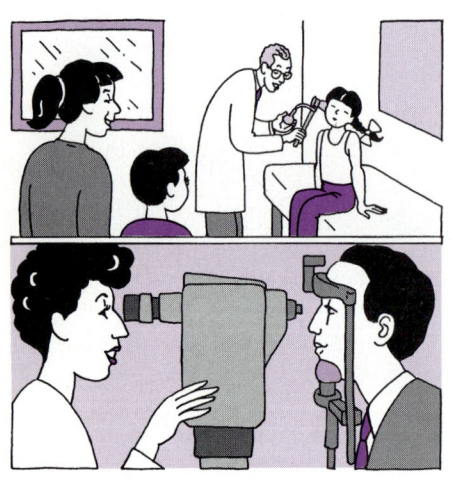

Mrs. Chin had to take her children to the doctor for a checkup last week. She takes them to a pediatrician, a doctor who treats only children. Her husband was having trouble with his eyes, so he went to a doctor who takes care only of eye problems. Many other doctors today specialize in only one branch of medicine—the medical problems of women, for example, or the heart, or even just the feet. In a hospital a surgeon performs operations, while an anesthetist administers the drug that stops the patient's pain. Even nurses specialize, with some who assist surgeons, some who deal only with children, and others who take care only of the elderly.

1. What did Mrs. Chin have to do last week?
2. To what kind of doctor does she take her children?
3. What kind of doctor did her husband go to?
4. What do many doctors today do?
5. What are some examples?
6. What does a surgeon do?
7. What does an anesthetist do?
8. What are some of the ways in which nurses specialize?

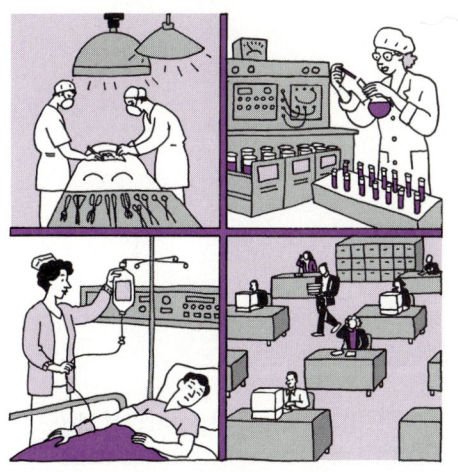

Medicine is a big business in the United States today. In fact, medicine is only one part of a giant industry that goes by the name of health care. It includes hospitals, clinics, laboratories, pharmacies, insurance companies, and government agencies. It employs not only doctors and dentists but also nurses, lab technicians, hospital orderlies, and thousands of office workers. The annual cost to the American public runs into billions of dollars.

9. Is medicine just a small business today?
10. What is medicine a part of?
11. What does the industry include?
12. Whom does it employ?
13. What is the annual cost to the American public?

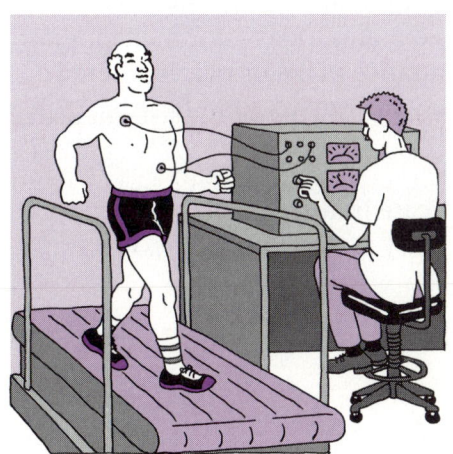

Jack McDonald had his annual checkup a few days ago. It used to be very simple—just a few tests, an X-ray of his lungs, and some questions from his doctor. This year there were a lot more tests, some of them on complex machines. It took twice as long, and it cost four times as much. Technology has improved medicine; it has helped doctors to diagnose illnesses more accurately and even to prolong life. On the other hand, it has increased the cost of medical services many times over. Much of this cost has been covered by insurance from both private companies and the government. Nevertheless, many people can no longer afford adequate health care.

14. What did Jack McDonald have a few days ago?
15. How did it used to be?
16. How was it this year?
17. What has improved medicine?
18. What has technology helped doctors to do?
19. What else has technology done?
20. How has much of the cost been covered?
21. Can everybody afford adequate health care?

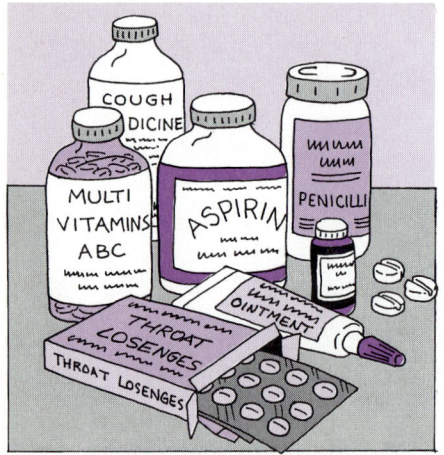

Doctors and hospitals are only part of the health care industry. The companies that make medicines are another important part of it. The American public spends billions of dollars every year on pills and other remedies. Some medicines can be obtained only with a doctor's prescription, but others are sold over the counter. If you don't eat properly, you can take a vitamin pill. If you have a headache, you can take an aspirin. If you have a cold, there are hundreds of different remedies that you can try. You can hardly get away from health care advertising in the United States today—for medicines or medical insurance plans or places where you can exercise your way to good health.

22. Of what are doctors and hospitals only a part?
23. What is another important part of the health care industry?
24. How much does the American public spend every year on medicines?
25. How must some medicines be obtained?
26. How are others sold?
27. What can you take if you don't eat properly?
28. What can you take if you have a headache?
29. What is there if you have a cold?
30. What can you hardly get away from in the United States today?
31. What are some of the things that are advertised?

B. Listen and repeat. Then answer the questions.

1. What do office workers have to do?
   They have to deal with a lot of paperwork every day.

2. What did she do with the old correspondence?
   She dealt with it by throwing it away.

3. Have you answered all the letters yet?
   I've dealt with all the easy ones, but I haven't started on the hard ones yet.

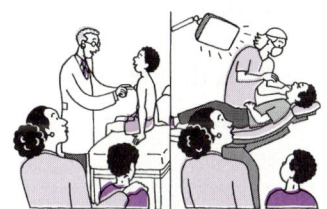

4. Does she take good care of the children's health?
   Yes, she has them checked twice a year not only by a pediatrician but also by a dentist.

5. Did that cold medicine help you?
   No, it didn't, but there are a lot of other remedies that I can get over the counter.

6. Do you have to have a prescription for all medicines in the United States?
   No. You can get things like aspirin or cold remedies over the counter, without a prescription.

7. How do they bend those steel rods?
   They bend them by machine.

8. How did he hurt his back?
   He hurt it when he bent over to pick up a heavy box.

9. Why are they letting her take so many courses this year?
   They've bent the rules a little so she can graduate this year.

10. Did you go to the hearing on the new property tax?
    They put it off for a week. This is the second time it's been postponed.

11. Why did they put off the meeting?
    They put it off because the sales manager was sick.

The irregular verbs *to deal (with)* and *to bend (over)* are introduced in this lesson.

> to deal–dealt–dealt
> to bend–bent–bent

C. Dialogue

Mr. and Mrs. Beck are getting ready to go to work.

MRS. BECK:	What's the matter with you this morning?
MR. BECK:	My back hurts. I can hardly bend over.
MRS. BECK:	You'd better go to see the doctor right away then.
MR. BECK:	Oh, I'll go to work and see whether I feel better.
MRS. BECK:	I don't think you should put it off.
MR. BECK:	I just had my annual checkup last week. This can't be anything serious because they checked me very carefully.
MRS. BECK:	But you look as if you're in pain right now.
MR. BECK:	Do we have anything I can take? An aspirin might help.
MRS. BECK:	An aspirin! That's not going to do any good.
MR. BECK:	It may help a little. Anyway, I can't afford to get sick.
MRS. BECK:	You're covered by your health insurance, aren't you?
MR. BECK:	That never takes care of all the expenses if you get really sick.
MRS. BECK:	Well, let's hope you're not that sick!
MR. BECK:	Don't you still have some of those pills you took after your operation last year?
MRS. BECK:	You shouldn't take those. They're very strong. I had to have a prescription for them.
MR. BECK:	If they're strong, they may be just what I need.
MRS. BECK:	They'd put you to sleep. You might fall asleep while you were driving to work.
MR. BECK:	Falling asleep sounds like the best idea of all. I think I'll just go back to bed. Then if I don't feel better tomorrow, I'll go to the doctor's.

Structure and Pattern Practice

Some adverbs of time are single words or expressions such as *yesterday, tomorrow, now, soon, last night, tomorrow afternoon.* Many others are prepositional phrases such as *at ten o'clock, in the winter, at noon, at night, in January, on Tuesday.* The most common position of adverbs of time is at the end of the sentence.

Health care has grown into a giant business in recent years.

There are a few single-word adverbs of place, such as *here, there, outside.* Most adverbs of place, however, are prepositional phrases, such as *at school, at home, in the house, on the table.* If a sentence contains both an adverb of place and an adverb of time, the adverb of place usually comes before the adverb of time.

They leave the correspondence on their desks at night.

A. Add the adverbial expression in parentheses at the correct place.

EXAMPLE

They leave the correspondence at night. (on their desks)

They leave the correspondence on their desks at night.

1. They want to settle down next year. (in New York)
2. She's going to start her job in the computer section. (on Monday)
3. She returned the books yesterday. (to the library)
4. He's working on an automobile assembly line. (this year)
5. They have to drive every day. (to the city)
6. I spent a week last year. (in the hospital)
7. She took the children to the pediatrician. (yesterday)
8. I had my checkup last week. (at the clinic)
9. She worked for many years. (in a factory)
10. We aren't going to discuss the budget at the meeting. (tomorrow)

Many adverbs of manner can be formed from adjectives by adding *ly.*

> She's a very careful driver.
> She drives very carefully.

Other adverbs of manner are:

accurately	pleasantly
dangerously	hungrily
beautifully	luckily

Note that final *y* changes to *i* before adding *ly.*

Other adverbs of manner, such as *fast, slow, well,* and *hard,* do not end in *ly.* The most common position for adverbs of manner is after the verb if there is no object, or after the object.

> She drives very carefully.
> She drove her car very carefully in the storm last night.

B. Complete with the adverbial form of the adjective in parentheses.

EXAMPLE

They connected the wires very _____ (careful)

They connected the wires very carefully.

1. They take vitamin pills because they don't eat _____ (proper).
2. The age of computers began only _____ (recent).
3. They must learn to do their work _____ (careful) in the computer section.
4. She passed all her exams _____ (easy).
5. I want to get reports from you _____ (regular).
6. She always speaks to everyone very _____ (pleasant).
7. The children looked at the food _____ (hungry).
8. Our corporation has grown very _____ (quick)
9. They give the workers a raise _____ (annual).
10. He had the accident because he was driving very _____ (dangerous).

Adverbs of frequency are words like always, *never, ever, often,* and *usually.* Their most common position is after *to be* but before other main verbs.

> The typists are always busy.
> They usually advertise in the newspapers.

Never and *hardly* are negatives so they are not used with *not.*

> I've never had trouble with my back before.
> They can hardly pay for a bottle of aspirin.

Ever is usually used in questions or with *not* in negative sentences.

> Has he ever studied mathematics?
> He hasn't ever studied mathematics.

C. Add the adverb of frequency at the correct place.

EXAMPLE

The bus is on time. (usually)

The bus is usually on time.

1. He has a checkup at a clinic. (always)
2. She buys pills over the counter. (never)
3. They hire workers without any experience. (often)
4. I haven't been interested in politics. (ever)
5. I can save a dollar. (hardly)
6. They advertise their products on television. (frequently)
7. I haven't driven my car in the city. (ever)
8. They try out the computer programs. (always)
9. They carry out the policies for the company. (generally)
10. I can balance my checkbook. (hardly ever)
11. The machines are out of order. (frequently)
12. The information that they give to management is important. (usually)

Pronunciation and Intonation Practice

A. Repeat several times.

b as in *bill*	*p* as in *put*	*f* as in *full*
bill	pill	fill
bull	pull	full
bit	pit	fit
beat	peat	feet
bad	pad	fad
bone	pone	phone
bar	par	far
bile	pile	file

B. Repeat these sentences.

1. I put the bill on top of that pile of files.
2. Please put a bit of peat on the fire.
3. The bill for that bit of food will be paid in full.
4. He's filled his pad with plants because that's the latest fad.
5. If I push and you pull, we can get this bag of pears off the truck.

C. Listen and repeat.

EXAMPLE

Let's hope you're not that sick!

1. I'm sure it isn't that bad!
2. It can't be that important!
3. The book wasn't that interesting!
4. It couldn't be that recent!
5. The exam wasn't that difficult!

General Practice

Conversation.

When did you have your last checkup? How often do you have one?

Do you get sick very often? If you do, what kind of illness?

What kinds of medicine do you take? For what?

Do you think it's a good idea for so many doctors to specialize in only one branch of medicine? Give your reasons.

Do you think government should take a bigger part in health care? Give your reasons.

Would you like to have a career in health care? What kind of career? Give your reasons.

Reading and Oral Practice

A. Listen and repeat. Then answer the questions.

Larry Nordstrom had been feeling run-down. He'd gained some weight, and he was tired all the time. His doctor finally told him that there wasn't anything seriously wrong with him. All he had to do was to watch his diet and get some regular exercise. Now Larry goes jogging every morning. He's been able to lose about ten pounds. He looks better, and he feels a lot better too.

1. How had Larry Nordstrom been feeling?
2. What was the matter with him?
3. What did his doctor finally tell him?
4. What did he have to do?
5. What does Larry do now?
6. What has he been able to do?
7. How does he look and feel?

"An ounce of prevention is worth a pound of cure," goes an old American saying. In other words, it's easier to prevent an illness than to cure it. Now that medical costs are so high, many Americans are working at staying healthy. Everywhere you go today, you see men and women running and jogging. A lot of others go to health clubs to work out on all kinds of muscle-building machines. Still others go in for sports in which they can participate, not just watch, sports like swimming and skiing, tennis and golf. "Fitness" has become a common word in the last few years. It includes all this emphasis on activities that help keep us in good health.

8. What is an old American saying?
9. What does it mean in other words?
10. Why are many Americans working at staying healthy?
11. What do you see everywhere you go?
12. What do a lot of others do?
13. What do still others do?
14. What are examples of sports in which people participate?
15. What has become a common word in the last few years?
16. What does it include?

SOME FOODS WITH CHOLESTEROL

Two other words that have become part of today's everyday vocabulary are "calories" and "cholesterol." A calorie is a measure of the energy that is produced by food. One way to control your weight is "to count calories"—that is, not to eat too much food and especially food that is too rich in calories. Cholesterol is a chemical that is found in animal fats. If you get too much of it in your food, it can damage your heart. People are now warned to stay away from, or at least to cut down on, foods like dairy products and red meats that are rich in cholesterol.

17. What are two other common words today?
18. What is a calorie?
19. What is one way to control your weight?
20. What does that mean?
21. What is cholesterol?
22. What happens if you get too much cholesterol?
23. What are people now warned to do?

NO SMOKING

Smoking has become the biggest "no" of all. The first thing that Larry's doctor told him to do was to give up cigarettes. Smoking damages the heart and lungs. It's bad not only for the person who smokes but for anyone who breathes in the smoke. Many places—offices, stores, theaters, restaurants, airplanes, for example—have prohibited smoking or set aside special areas for it. So eat properly, get regular exercise, stop smoking—and stay healthy!

24. What has smoking become?
25. What was the first thing Larry's doctor told him to do?
26. What does smoking do?
27. Is smoking bad only for the person who smokes?
28. What have many places done?
29. What are examples of some of them?
30. What can you do to stay healthy?

1. Why is she going to see her doctor?
   She's been feeling very run-down. She's lost a lot of weight, she has headaches, and she's tired.

2. What sports did he go in for in college?
   He went in for all the ones where he could get a lot of exercise.

3. Why does he go to the health club so often?
   He goes there to work out. He lifts weights so he'll get stronger.

4. What have they warned the workers?
   They've warned them to stay away from those dangerous machines.

5. What are all these new rules that they've issued?
   They're supposed to help us cut down on our paperwork.

6. Have you given up smoking?
   Yes, I gave it up last year.

7. Have they set aside this area for something special?
   Yes, they've set it aside for people who still smoke.

C. Dialogue

Rita and Dave have just finished dinner at a restaurant.

RITA: That was a good dinner.

DAVE: Yes, it was. Are you going to have coffee?

RITA: No, I don't think so. My doctor told me to cut down on it.

DAVE: Shall we go then?

RITA: Oh, look at that dessert over there! Doesn't it look just wonderful!

DAVE: It looks rich. Too rich.

RITA: Yes, I suppose so. A thousand calories.

DAVE: Two thousand is more like it. Look at all that cream.

RITA: Yes, I suppose it's full of cholesterol. Isn't it too bad?

DAVE: Isn't what too bad?

RITA: That we have to stay away from all the things we really like—desserts, coffee, cigarettes.

DAVE: But you feel better for staying away from them, don't you? You certainly look better.

RITA: Yes, it's true. I *have* started to lose a little weight.

DAVE: Yes, I can see that.

RITA: About five pounds so far. The doctor said I had to lose ten, so I'm halfway there.

DAVE: And what about smoking?

RITA: I haven't had a cigarette for two weeks. It hasn't been too hard to give up smoking.

DAVE: Great! Now how about coming out jogging with me tomorrow morning?

RITA: Oh, I don't think I'm quite ready for *that*.

Structure and Pattern Practice

One of the most common kinds of English verbs is the multiple-word verb, a verb to which a preposition or adverb has been added so that the meaning changes:

look	turn	get
look at	turn on	get on
look for	turn off	get up

With some of these verbs, the verb and the word that follows it cannot be separated.

He's looking at the newspaper now.
I was listening to the teacher.

With many others, however, the verb and the following word can be separated.

She filled out the application.
She filled the application out before she left the office.

A. Change the sentences so that the parts of the two-word verbs are separated.

EXAMPLE

I'll turn on the lights in a few minutes.

I'll turn the lights on in a few minutes.

1. The merchants set up their stalls in the market.
2. I have to fill out this application today.
3. They turn out the cars on an assembly line.
4. They tore down those houses to make space for a new office building.
5. She brought back the books.
6. The new management took over the company last month.
7. They'll need to fix up the house before they can move in.
8. He set aside the difficult letters until another day.

B. Change these sentences so that the two parts of the two-word verbs are *not* separated.

He turned the radio off.

He turned off the radio.

1. I want to try the car out before I buy it.
2. They brought their children up in a small town.
3. I've picked all my clothes up.
4. He threw the sports section away.
5. The bank lends some money out to students.
6. We put our books down.
7. They've put the meeting off for another day.
8. We shipped the packages out yesterday afternoon.

With separable verbs, the two parts *must* be separated when the object is a personal pronoun.

I'm going to fill out these forms tomorrow.
I'm going to fill them out tomorrow

I turned off the air conditioner.
I turned it off because it was getting too cold in here.

C. Change the object to the appropriate personal pronoun and then separate the two parts of the two-word verbs.

I put on my hat.

I put it on.

1. They've put off the public hearing for another week.
2. He calls up his wife at noon every day.
3. She's taken off her coat.
4. They send out all the letters every afternoon.
5. You don't need to fill out these forms.
6. She carried out the policies very carefully.

7. They want to build up the business.
8. You can drop off these packages at the post office on your way home.
9. He makes up the lesson plan before class every day.
10. The firefighters put out the fire in a few minutes.
11. He's going to set up his own business next year.
12. I forgot to turn out the lights.
13. She has to give up rich desserts if she wants to lose weight.
14. They'll turn off the electricity if you don't pay your bill.
15. When did he pay off his debts?

Pronunciation and Intonation Practice

A. Repeat several times.

d as in *did*	*th* as in *thing*	*s* as in *sick*
Dick	thick	sick
din	thin	sin
dank	thank	sank
ding	thing	sing
dumb	thumb	sum
deem	theme	seem
die	thigh	sigh

B. Repeat these sentences.

1. On her desk I saw the thesis that she'd written.
2. Dick is so thin that I think he must be sick.
3. The things that they do are making them sick.
4. Did you thank Donna for singing that song?
5. He sucked on his thumb while he tried to do his sums.

C. Listen and repeat.

At least it would be our own.

1. You'll need your own.
2. I offered her my umbrella, but she wants her own.
3. He has some money of his own.
4. Here's your book, but I can't find my own.
5. They won't have to buy all their food at the store. They can grow their own.

General Practice

Conversation.

Do you think you should get regular checkups or wait to see a doctor until you get sick? Give your reasons.

Do you think it's important to get regular exercise? Give your reasons.

Do you get enough exercise? What do you do?

What kind of sports do you like to watch? Which ones do you participate in?

Have you ever had to lose (or gain) weight? What did you do about it?

Do you smoke? Have you ever tried to stop? Was it easy or difficult?

Do you think people should be allowed to smoke any place that they want? Give your reasons.

Reading and Oral Practice

A. Listen and repeat. Then answer the questions.

Cathy Lewis was in tenth grade when she had to transfer to a new school. It wasn't a change to a nearby school; it was all the way across the country. Her father's company had transferred him from Oregon to New Jersey, almost three thousand miles away. Cathy was scared the first few days in her new school. She expected everything to be strange and different. Instead she found the courses were just about the same as those she had been studying before. Two of the textbooks were even the same as she'd used back in Oregon.

1. What happened to Cathy Lewis when she was in tenth grade?
2. Was her new school near her old school?
3. What had her father's company done?
4. How was Cathy in her first few days in her new school?
5. How did she expect everything to be?
6. What did she find instead?
7. Were all her textbooks different from her old ones?

Schools in the United States are controlled by local governments; nevertheless, school systems throughout the country are very similar. The normal school system consists of six years of elementary school and six of high school. In many districts, high school is divided into three years of junior high and three of senior high. Each school year is called a grade—the ninth grade, for example, is the last year of junior high in most localities. In addition, almost all school systems have a year of kindergarten for children too young for first grade. Education is compulsory—that is, it is required by law—everywhere in the country. However, the age at which a child can leave school differs from place to place. The average throughout the country is about sixteen.

8. Are schools in the United States controlled by the federal government?
9. Are school systems throughout the country very different?
10. What does the normal school system consist of?
11. How is high school divided in many districts?
12. What is each school year called? What is an example?
13. What else do almost all school systems have?
14. What is compulsory education?
15. Can a child leave school at the same age everywhere in the country?
16. What is the average age at which a child can leave school?

While the curriculum is more or less the same everywhere, the quality of the schools is often very unequal. Some areas have far more money to spend for each pupil each year. In general, schools in suburban communities are better than those in either large cities or rural areas. In addition to the public schools, there are a number of private schools. In the public schools, education is free, but private schools charge a fee, sometimes a very high one.

17. Which differs more from area to area, the curriculum or the quality of the schools?
18. What is one reason the quality of schools is unequal?
19. Where are schools better in general?
20. Are public schools the only schools in the United States?
21. In what kind of schools is education free?
22. What kind of school charges a fee?

GRADUATE SCHOOL
YALE UNIVERSITY

There are also both public and private universities. The most famous American universities—Harvard, Yale, and Princeton, for example—are private, but some of the largest universities are public. California operates a university system with branches all over the state. The entire system has about a hundred and fifty thousand students. To teach the millions of students at all levels of the American educational system, there are more than two million teachers. In fact, they make up the largest single group of government employees in the country.

23. Are all universities public?
24. What are some of the most famous American universities? Are they public or private?
25. What state has a large public university system?
26. How many students does the system have?
27. How many teachers are there in the American educational system?
28. What do all these teachers make up?

1. Do people speak the same way all over the United States?
Speech patterns differ from region to region, but not a great deal.

2. Why was it so difficult for her to learn Spanish?
Because it was so different from her own language.

3. Do they like the food here?
No, not too much. It's too different from the food in their own country.

4. Is his new car the same color as his old one?
It's similar to the old one, but not exactly the same.

5. Do you have enough time to finish all the work?
Yes, we have far more than we need.

6. What do you want more than anything else?
I wish I had my college degree so I could go out and start working right away.

7. Where would you like to be today?
   I wish I were at the beach right now.

8. What's the matter with you today?
   I'm very tired. I wish that I'd stayed home
   last night.

9. Why isn't he doing well at work?
   He can't get used to following all the
   new regulations.

10. Where are the children?
    I sent all the kids outside to play.

Note that in clauses following the verb *to wish,* which is
introduced in this lesson, the same verb forms are used as in
contrary-to-fact conditions. The past tense is the present
contrary-to-fact form and the past perfect is the past contrary-to-
fact form. As in present contrary-to-fact conditions, the form of
to be used with all persons is *were.*

> I wish I knew the answer.
> I wish he were working already.
> He wished he'd had a car for his date that night.

Note also that *different* is followed by *from* when a noun or
pronoun comes after.

> Our schools were very different from theirs.

Kid is a colloquial expression for *child.*

C. Dialogue

Danny introduces himself to Cathy in the school cafeteria.

DANNY: Hi. You're new here, aren't you?

CATHY: Yes, I just started this semester.

DANNY: May I sit down?

CATHY: Yes, please. My name is Cathy.

DANNY: Mine's Danny. Where did you go to school before?

CATHY: In Oregon.

DANNY: Oregon! That's *really* a long way from here! This must be pretty strange.

CATHY: No, I was surprised, the schools are a lot alike. All my courses are about the same. We're even using the same texts in Spanish and social studies.

DANNY: I had to change schools when I was in third grade. Of course I was only a kid then, but I still missed the old place for a long time.

CATHY: Oh, sometimes I wish I were back home. There, you see! I was thinking of Oregon as home.

DANNY: You'll get used to things around here pretty soon.

CATHY: Yes, I'm sure I will. I've already started to make a few friends.

DANNY: It helps if you go out for an extracurricular activity, you know, like the band or something like that.

CATHY: I've already joined the drama club.

DANNY: Yeah, that's a good choice. You'll meet a lot of kids there.

CATHY: What about you? What do you belong to?

DANNY: Well, I don't have time for any of them.

CATHY: Really? Why not?

DANNY: Well, see, I'm on the football team. I have to practice every afternoon.

CATHY: But I'm sure you'd be a good actor. You should come around to the drama club.

Structure and Pattern Practice

The indefinite or impersonal pronouns are:

someone	anyone	no one	everyone
somebody	anybody	nobody	everybody
something	anything	nothing	everything

Like *some* and *any*, the indefinite pronouns are affirmatively and negatively distributed. The *no* words can be used in place of *not any*.

> I saw someone at the tax bureau.
> I didn't see anyone at the tax bureau.
> I saw no one at the tax bureau.

Only one negative at a time is used with an English verb, so be careful not to use the *no* words with another negative.

The indefinite pronouns are singular and are followed by third person singular verb forms.

> Nobody was in the office when I came in.
> Everything that you need is on your desk.

None means *not one*. It is frequently used in partitive constructions with *of*. It also is followed by third person singular verb forms.

> None of the typists has come in yet.
> None of the newspapers gives me all the information I need.

A. Change the negative from *not any* to words with *no*.

EXAMPLE

There isn't anybody in the office today.

There's nobody in the office today.

1. I don't have anything to do.
2. There isn't anything interesting in the newspaper today.
3. I don't know anyone who wants to go into politics.
4. They haven't asked anyone to fill that position yet.
5. I can't find anybody who'll help me.
6. She didn't have anything to say to him.

The *any* words can be used in affirmative sentences in the sense of *no matter who, no matter what.*

Anyone in the office (no matter who) can help you.

The *no* words are the negatives for the any words when they are used in this sense.

Anyone can answer the question.
No one can answer the question.

B. Change to the negative with the appropriate *no* word.

Anyone can answer your question.

No one can answer your question.

1. Anybody can take over my job.
2. Anyone can fix this machine.
3. Anybody can balance a checkbook.
4. Anybody can fill out that application.
5. Anything in the store can be bought with a credit card.
6. Anyone can understand this problem.

C. Change to the affirmative with the appropriate *any* word.

Nobody can stay in the building after five.

Anybody can stay in the building after five.

1. Nothing you do is okay with me.
2. Nobody can depend on that information.
3. Nothing you do will bother me.
4. No one can find that information.
5. Nobody can work with him.
6. Nothing that you try will work.

Many other expressions are normally used in either affirmative or negative sentences but not in both.

Affirmative	Negative
some	any
a lot of	many
a lot of/a great deal of	much
a long way	far
too (meaning also)	either
already	yet
still anymore	

Much and *many* are used in affirmative sentences when they come before the verb.

> Much paper is used by the government.
> Many students have to change schools in the middle of the year.

D. Change to the negative.

EXAMPLE

I know someone who has a government job.

I don't know anyone who has a government job.

1. She had something to tell me.
2. She's still in the training program.
3. She's already joined the drama club.
4. He had to ask someone to balance his checkbook.
5. It's a long way from my home to the university.
6. The university gives a lot of scholarships.
7. My friend is a government employee too.
8. I've already filled out the application.
9. She's still putting her money in a checking account.
10. That job gives them a lot of security.
11. They've already recommended somebody for that job.
12. The government has already collected the taxes for the year.
13. There were a lot of passengers on the plane.
14. It's a long way from the hotel to the beach.
15. He's still working in the factory.

16. I depend on someone to help me.
17. She wants to study mathematics too.
18. There are a lot of new employees in the training program.
19. They have a lot of maintenance to do on those machines.
20. She still uses her credit card for every purchase.

Pronunciation and Intonation Practice

A. Repeat several times.

th as in *they*	*d* as in *day*
they	day
then	den
there	dare
those	doze

z as in *zoo*	*d* as in *day*
zoo	due
zeal	deal
zip	dip
zed	dead

B. Repeat these sentences.

1. Those girls didn't go to the zoo that day.
2. They saw a zebra on the day that they went to the zoo.
3. I'll doze for a while and then we'll zip over there for a dip.
4. The lazy lads are due for a zero on their exams.
5. The lad zooms around from this to that all the day long.

EXAMPLE

You can't have that much of a pain!

1. There can't be that many jobs available!
2. They can't offer that many courses!
3. You shouldn't take that much medicine!
4. They couldn't have had that many new employees!
5. We don't have that much time!

General Practice

Conversation.

At what age do children start school in your country?

How many years does a child spend in elementary school in your country? In high school?

Is education compulsory in your country? To what age?

Are the schools in your country better in some areas than in others? What makes some of them better?

Are there private schools in your country? Which are better, the private schools or the public?

Are the universities in your country public or private?

Is education in your country controlled by the national government or by local governments?

Which do you think is better, local government or national government control of schools? Give your reasons.

Reading and Oral Practice

A. Listen and repeat. Then answer the questions.

There's another American saying, "All work and no play makes Jack a dull boy." But Jack, and Jill too, now do have more than enough time for play—leisure-time activities, to use the current expression. Most Americans work only forty hours a week. They have evenings and weekends free to enjoy themselves. There are also a few long weekends during the year since some holidays now fall on Monday. In addition, many men and women have two or more weeks of vacation time every year. Thousands of people work at filling up all this leisure time; they work while others play.

1. What is another American saying?
2. What do most men and women now have?
3. What is a current expression for the things we do as play?
4. How many hours do most Americans work?
5. When are they free to enjoy themselves?
6. Why are there a few long weekends during the year?
7. What else do many men and women have?
8. What do thousands of people work at?

Not so many years ago, people used to have to go out for entertainment if they didn't stay home and read. They could go to the movies, the theater, the ballpark, wherever there was something happening. Now they can stay home, but instead of curling up with a good book, they usually watch television. Television brings not only the latest news but also just about anything you can imagine in the way of entertainment right into your home. You can see movies, concerts, entertainment programs, and spectator sports like football, basketball, and baseball without getting up from your chair. Only a few thousand people can watch a football game right there in the stadium, but millions can see it on TV. And now you can see movies only a year or so old on a VCR.

9. What did people have to do for entertainment not so many years ago?
10. Where could they go for entertainment?
11. What can they do now?
12. What does television bring right into your home?
13. What can you see on television?
14. How many people can see a football game in the stadium? On TV?
15. What can you see on a VCR?

Television is a very passive kind of entertainment—you just sit and watch the little screen. There are, however, still a lot of other pastimes that require active participation, like some of the sports that we've already mentioned. They're not only good for your health but fun too. We've also talked about tourism; it keeps growing because so many people are getting more vacation time. Tourists flock to places where there are natural attractions—beautiful scenery, beaches, lakes, mountains. Where they do not exist, attractions such as amusement parks, luxury hotels, and of course places to shop have been created.

16. Why is television a passive kind of entertainment?
17. What do a lot of other pastimes require?
18. Are some of the sports that have been mentioned good only for your health?
19. Why does tourism keep growing?
20. Where do tourists flock?
21. What has been created where natural attractions do not exist?

Hobbies are another way in which people can fill up their leisure time. A hobby is just something that someone likes to do away from work. Some people collect stamps or watch birds, others go hunting or fishing. Many men and women are amateur artists; that is, they aren't trying to make their living in the arts. They paint pictures, play a musical instrument, or make pottery just for their own enjoyment. That's what leisure time is for—to get away from work and to enjoy yourself.

22. What is another way in which people can fill up their leisure time?
23. What is a hobby?
24. What are some of the things people do?
25. What are many men and women?
26. Do amateurs make their living in the arts?
27. What do these people do?
28. What is leisure time for?

1. What day is your birthday going to be?
   It falls on a Tuesday this year.

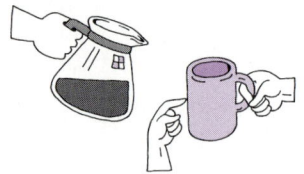

2. There's more coffee. Do you want me to fill up your cup?
   Just fill it up halfway please.

3. Are you going to watch TV tonight?
   No, I'm not. I got a book out of the library today, and I'm going to curl up with it and spend the evening reading.

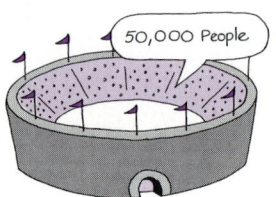

4. How many people can the stadium hold?
   It can hold fifty thousand or so, I don't know exactly.

5. Is she a professional artist?
   No, she isn't. She makes her living as a lawyer.

6. What are we going to do about dinner tonight?
   I really don't have anything in mind. I haven't planned anything.

TIM: What are we going to do?

NORA: We have a lot of errands to take care of on the long weekend, you know that. Groceries, laundry, cleaning the house.

TIM: Oh, we're not going to spend the whole weekend on that kind of nonsense.

NORA: Well, is there anything special on television?

TIM: And I'm not going to sit around staring at a little screen for three days.

NORA: We could rent some movies and watch them on the VCR. The one that was such a big hit last year—what was it called?—has just come out.

TIM: No, no, no! I want to get out! I want to get some fresh air!

NORA: Well, the grass needs cutting.

TIM: You know I don't mean that. Now wait a minute! I see what you're doing. You already have something in mind.

NORA: Well, yes, I do.

TIM: So what is it?

NORA: Don't you think it would be nice to take a little trip?

TIM: That's just what I was going to suggest. But of course you've already decided where we should go.

NORA: Well, I have an idea.

TIM: Well, go on, tell me.

NORA: There's a new hotel up in the mountains. We can just lie around and rest, or we can play tennis or go swimming. And do a little shopping too. The hotel has everything.

TIM: All right, what's it called? I'll call and see if we can get a reservation.

NORA: Oh, I've already done that.

Structure and Pattern Practice

> Auxiliary verbs are often used in English in order to avoid repeating some verb or verb phrase used earlier in the sentence. If there is no auxiliary earlier in the sentence, the auxiliary *do*, *does*, or *did* is used as a substitute verb. Note the following examples where auxiliary verbs are used with *too* for this purpose.
>
> Helen painted a picture, and I painted a picture.
> Helen painted a picture, and I did too.
>
> Martin likes to watch TV, and Sylvia likes to watch TV.
> Martin likes to watch TV, and Sylvia does too.

A. Change the second part of each sentence so that it has an auxiliary verb and *too*.

EXAMPLE

She studies English, and I study English.

She studies English, and I do too.

1. My mother enjoyed the movie, and my father enjoyed the movie.
2. They've bought a VCR, and we've bought a VCR.
3. Sylvia plays a musical instrument, and Martin plays a musical instrument.
4. We'll go for a trip this weekend, and our friends will go for a trip this weekend.
5. She has a checking account, and her husband has a checking account.
6. The furniture store advertised a sale, and the clothing store advertised a sale.

> *So* can also be used with an auxiliary verb for the same purpose. Note, however, that with *so*, the auxiliary verb comes before the subject.
>
> Helen painted a picture, and I painted a picture.
> Helen painted a picture, and so did I.

B. Change the second part of each sentence so that it uses an auxiliary verb and *so*.

E X A M P L E

She studies English, and I study English.

She studies English, and so do I.

1. I got a letter, and Bill got a letter.
2. I've given them some money, and my husband has given them some money.
3. I bought a ticket to the concert, and my wife bought a ticket to the concert.
4. You can go to the movie, and John can go to the movie.
5. I must pass all the exams, and you must pass all the exams.
6. She attends a lot of meetings, and I attend a lot of meetings.

In the negative, either is used instead of too in shortened sentences.

I didn't get a raise, and my friend didn't get a raise.
I didn't get a raise, and my friend didn't either.

C. Change the second part of each sentence so that it uses an auxiliary verb and *either*.

E X A M P L E

I didn't like the movie, and Bill didn't like the movie.

I didn't like the movie, and Bill didn't either.

1. She can't go to the movies, and her sister can't go to the movies.
2. I haven't read the newspaper, and my wife hasn't read the newspaper.
3. You won't enjoy yourself, and I won't enjoy myself.
4. They don't have a savings account, and we don't have a savings account.
5. I shouldn't talk in class, and you shouldn't talk in class.
6. He hadn't graduated from college, and his friend hadn't graduated from college.

> *Neither* can also be used in shortened negative
> sentences. The word order with *neither* is the same
> as with *so*.
>
> > I didn't get a raise, and my friend didn't get a raise.
> > I didn't get a raise, and neither did my friend.

D. Change the second part of each sentence so that it uses an auxiliary
verb and *neither*.

I didn't like the movie, and Bill didn't like the movie.

I didn't like the movie, and neither did Bill.

1. I don't watch television very often, and my husband doesn't
   watch television very often.
2. I've never seen a football game, and my friends have never seen a
   football game.
3. My sister doesn't like popular music, and I don't like popular music.
4. He isn't sure of the amount, and I'm not sure of the amount.
5. They mustn't walk on the grass, and we mustn't walk on the grass.
6. I won't fill out the forms, and she won't fill out the forms.

> Auxiliary verbs are also used alone in so-called
> balanced sentences, where the second clause
> describes a situation which is the opposite of that
> described in the first clause. An auxiliary verb is
> used in the second clause to avoid repetition of
> the verb or verb phrase in the first clause.
>
> > Sylvia doesn't like to dance, but I do.
> > Harold is going to get a scholarship,
> >   but John isn't.

E. Change the second part of each sentence so that it uses only the subject and an auxiliary verb.

I like to watch TV, but my wife doesn't like to watch TV.

I like to watch TV, but my wife doesn't.

1. We didn't take a trip, but our friends took a trip.
2. I understood the lesson, but John didn't understand the lesson.
3. John won't lend you any money, but I'll lend you some money.
4. I've never been to New York, but my brother has been to New York.
5. Jane called me, but Maria didn't call me.
6. Harold doesn't read a lot, but Jane reads a lot.

Pronunciation and Intonation Practice

A. Repeat several times.

d as in *bad*	*t* as in *at*
ad	at
bad	bat
bed	bet
seed	seat

g as in *big*	*ck* as in *luck*
bag	back
rag	rack
lag	lack
lug	luck

B. Repeat these sentences.

1. The lad sat on a big bag at the back of the truck.
2. He had a big rug that he'd put in a bag at the back of the truck.
3. We tried to find a big bed, but we had no luck at all.
4. He had tied the bag on his back with a bit of string.
5. The back of the bag had a tag that gave the date.

C. Listen and repeat.

EXAMPLE

She wants to go, and so do I.

1. She studies art, and so do I.
2. They like music, and we do too.
3. She doesn't want to stay home, and I don't either.
4. He doesn't have a scholarship, and neither do I.
5. They enjoyed the movie, and we did too.

General Practice

Conversation.

How many hours do you work (or attend school)? How much time does this leave you for leisure time activities?

How much vacation time do you have every year? What do you do with it?

What holidays are there during the year? Which of them make long weekends?

How much time do you spend watching television? Which would you rather do, go out to a movie or stay home and watch TV? Give your reasons.

What kinds of entertainment in addition to TV are available in your country or region? Which ones do you enjoy?

Reading and TV are both passive kinds of entertainment. In what ways do you think they're different from each other?

Do you have a hobby? What is it? How much time do you spend on it?

Would you like to have a career in the arts or in the entertainment business? Give your reasons.

Structure and Pattern Practice

A. Add the adverbial expression in parentheses in the correct place in these sentences.

They leave the correspondence at night. (on their desks)

They leave the correspondence on their desks at night.

1. They sold a lot of merchandise. (last year)
2. They go jogging in the morning. (always)
3. He bought some pills yesterday. (at the pharmacy)
4. I don't feel sick. (ever)
5. They study the lesson every day. (carefully)
6. That doctor takes care only of young children. (usually)
7. He filled out the application. (never)
8. I walk to work. (every morning)
9. They bought a small house last year. (in the suburbs)
10. They stay at a hotel in the city. (frequently)
11. He'll be an amateur. (always)
12. They had a meeting Friday afternoon. (in the office)
13. They checked his health last week. (carefully)
14. He performs his job. (always) (carefully)
15. I saw them last night. (at a restaurant)
16. There are changes in government regulations. (often)

B. Change the following sentences so that the two parts of the two-word verbs are separated.

I'll turn on the lights in a few minutes.

I'll turn the lights on in a few minutes.

1. They expect the ads to bring in more business.
2. You can't throw away that picture.
3. She spread out the newspaper on the floor.
4. I smashed up the car one night in a storm.
5. She called up her friends from the phone in the office.
6. He'll pay off his debts within a year.
7. She filled out the application yesterday.
8. A new management group is going to take over the company.
9. You have to bring in the groceries now.
10. They put aside the merchandise for a sale.

C. Change the object to the appropriate personal pronoun and then separate the two parts of the two-word verbs.

I put on my hat.

I put it on.

1. He set up his own business last year.
2. She set aside the newspaper until she could read it carefully.
3. She calls up her husband every morning when she gets to work.
4. They've put off the concert for another week.
5. After they bought their new car, they picked up his mother to show it to her.
6. He says he'll give up smoking next month.
7. They're going to tear down these buildings.
8. He turned off the radio because he couldn't study.
9. I'll pay off my debts next month.
10. I haven't filled out the forms yet.

D. Change the negative from *not any* to *no.*

There isn't anybody in the office today.

Therre's nobody in the office today.

1. He didn't have any work experience.
2. There weren't any shops in the hotel.
3. I couldn't find any fresh oranges in the store.
4. I didn't learn anything in that course.
5. They can't find anyone who'll take care of their children.
6. You can't depend on anybody to help you.
7. We haven't had any rain this month.
8. There isn't anything I can tell you.
9. They haven't trained anybody to replace her.
10. I haven't seen anything that I wanted to see.

E. Change to the negative with the appropriate no word.

Anyone can answer your question.

No one can answer your question.

1. Anything will be successful.
2. Anybody will take this report seriously.
3. Anyone can understand the new regulations.
4. Anybody can fix up that old house.
5. Anyone can give management all the information they need.
6. Anything can improve these roads.
7. Anybody will lend you the money you need.
8. Anything can replace the old regulations.
9. Anyone can handle that job.
10. Anybody can influence his decisions.

F. Change to the negative.

EXAMPLE

I know someone who has a government job.

I don't know anyone who has a government job.

1. He knows how to play golf too.
2. After he took the pills, he was still in pain.
3. She's already made a reservation
4. They have a lot of laundry to do.
5. There are a lot of tourists staying in the hotel.
6. I saw some pictures that I liked.
7. I've already cut down on cholesterol.
8. They have a lot of paperwork in that office.
9. It's a long way from the farm to the nearest town.
10. We have to do a lot of errands on Saturday.
11. It's a long way from their house to the center of the city.
12. He's still working out at the health club every day.
13. She has something important to do.
14. They've already announced her promotion.
15. My boss has a lot of influence with management.
16. There were a lot of people in the stadium for the game yesterday.
17. They've already bought a VCR.
18. I'm still thinking about changing jobs.
19. I have a long way to go to my office.
20. They like to go hunting too.

G. Change the second part of each sentence so that it uses the appropriate auxiliary verb and *too* or *either*.

EXAMPLE

She studies English, and I study English.

She studies English, and I do too.

1. The children like milk, and I like milk.
2. She doesn't drink coffee, and her husband doesn't drink coffee.
3. He's a blue-collar worker, and his brother is a blue-collar worker.
4. I haven't seen the budget, and she hasn't seen the budget.
5. He forgot to turn off the lights, and I forgot to turn off the lights.
6. She didn't have any technical experience, and I didn't have any technical experience.
7. I can't answer the question, and you can't answer the question.
8. I do a lot of maintenance work, and she does a lot of maintenance work.

H. Change the second part of each sentence so that it uses the appropriate auxiliary verb and *so* or *neither*.

EXAMPLE

She studies English, and I study English.

She studies English, and so do I.

1. I eat in a cafeteria every day, and she eats in a cafeteria every day.
2. I need to take a vacation, and you need to take a vacation.
3. She hasn't had lunch yet, and he hasn't had lunch yet.
4. He isn't interested in technical work, and I'm not interested in technical work.
5. The blue-collar workers didn't obtain a raise, and the white-collar workers didn't obtain a raise.
6. She's a member of the union, and her husband is a member of the union.
7. The spark plugs haven't been installed, and the carburetor hasn't been installed.
8. I should visit that resort, and you should visit that resort.

General Practice

Tanya Barsamian wants to be an actor. She appeared in several plays for her high school and college drama clubs. She felt that she was good enough to make a career in the professional theater. Her friends also believed that she had a future in the theater or the movies. Because New York is the most important center for the arts in the United States, she finally decided to move there. She has a very busy life now. She has to work as a waitress to pay the rent for her tiny apartment. She also attends drama and dancing classes. In addition she tries out for every play, movie, or TV program that is being produced in New York. Last week she got lucky. She got a small part in a TV film that will be made in New York. She hopes that she will attract enough attention to get more parts.

1. What does Tanya Barsamian want to be?
2. What did she appear in?
3. What did she feel?
4. What did her friends believe?
5. Why did she decide to move to New York?
6. What kind of life does she have now?
7. Why does she work as a waitress?
8. What kind of classes does she attend?
9. What does she do in addition?
10. What happened to her last week?
11. What did she get?
12. What does she hope?

B. Conversation.

Do you think it's easy or difficult to get good health care? Give your reasons.

How do you think health care can be improved?

What do you do to stay healthy?

Do you think local government or the national government should be in charge of education? Give your reasons.

How do you think education in your country (or region) can be improved?

What kind of entertainment do you enjoy most?

So you think people have too much or not enough leisure time? Give your reasons.

Would you like to have a career in health care? Give your reasons.

Would you like to have a career in education? Give your reasons.

Would you like to have a career in the arts or in the entertainment business? Give your reasons.

Vocabulary

The following list includes the words introduced in Book 5. The number indicates the page on which the word first appears. If a word can be used as more than one part of speech, the way it is used in the book is as follows: n = noun, v = verb, aux = auxiliary verb, adj = adjective, pron = pronoun, prep = preposition, poss = possessive, interj = interjection, intens = intensifier. If a word has more than one meaning or is part of a longer word or expression, the meaning or complete expression used in the book will be in parentheses.

ability, 23
account, 51
accountant, 23
accurately, 97
acre, 13
action, 22
active, 128
actor, 121
add (v), 12
adequate, 97
administer (v), 70
administration, 23
adventure, 60
advertisement, 34
against, 60
age, 117
agency, 21
air conditioning, 2
air force, 71
alike, 121
allow (v), 41 note
amateur, 129
ambulance, 70
among, 34
amount, 52
amusement, 128
anesthetist, 96
animal, 108
announce (v), 16
annual, 97
anymore, 124 note
appliance, 1
application, 74

army, 71
artist, 129
aside, 36
aspirin, 98
assemble (v), 11
assembly (line/plant), 12
assist (v), 96
attention, 80
attraction, 61
availability, 12
average, 117
avoid (v), 60

baker, 33
balance (v), 54
ballpark, 128
band, 121
baseball, 128
basis, 59
bend (over) (v), 100
besides, 63
beyond, 70
bill, 54
billion, 97
bird, 129
blue-collar, 3
bookkeeper, 22
boring, 74
box, 100
brakes, 1
bring in (v), 36
budget, 1

bureau, 71
bureaucrat, 71
butcher, 33

calorie, 108
camel, 60
carburetor, 11
carefully, 101
carry out (v), 22
cash, 51
change (n), 26
charge (v), 51
charge account, 52
cheaply, 12
checkbook, 54
checking account, 51
checkup, 96
choice, 121
cholesterol, 108
cigarette, 109
clinic, 97
combine (v), 59
common, 108
communications, 59
complex, 11
compulsory, 117
consider (v), 3
consist (of) (v), 11
constant, 61
consumer, 11
contact (with) (v), 69
contract, 50

Irregular Verbs

Principal Parts of Irregular Verbs

INFINITIVE	PAST	PAST PARTICIPLE
to be (is, am, are)	was, were	been
to become	became	become
to begin	began	begun
to bend	bent	bent
to blow	blew	blown
to break	broke	broken
to bring	brought	brought
to build	built	built
to buy	bought	bought
to catch	caught	caught
to choose	chose	chosen
to come	came	come
to cost	cost	cost
to cut	cut	cut
to deal	dealt	dealt
to dig	dug	dug
to do	did	done
to draw	drew	drawn
to drink	drank	drunk
to drive	drove	driven
to eat	ate	eaten
to fall	fell	fallen
to feel	felt	felt
to find	found	found
to fly	flew	flown
to forget	forgot	forgotten
to freeze	froze	frozen
to get	got	gotten
to give	gave	given
to go	went	gone
to grow	grew	grown
to hang	hung	hung
to have	had	had

INFINITIVE	PAST	PAST PARTICIPLE
to hear	heard	heard
to hold	held	held
to hurt	hurt	hurt
to keep	kept	kept
to know	knew	known
to lead	led	led
to leave	left	left
to lend	lent	lent
to let	let	let
to lie	lay	lain
to lose	lost	lost
to make	made	made
to mean	meant	meant
to meet	met	met
to pay	paid	paid
to put	put	put
to quit	quit	quit
to read	read	read
to ride	rode	ridden
to ring	rang	rung
to rise	rose	risen
to run	ran	run
to say	said	said
to see	saw	seen
to sell	sold	sold
to send	sent	sent
to set	set	set
to shake	shook	shaken
to show	showed	shown
to sing	sang	sung
to sit	sat	sat
to sleep	slept	slept
to speak	spoke	spoken
to spend	spent	spent
to spread	spread	spread
to spring	sprang	sprung
to stand	stood	stood
to swim	swam	swum
to take	took	taken
to teach	taught	taught
to tear	tore	torn
to tell	told	told

INFINITIVE	PAST	PAST PARTICIPLE
to think	thought	thought
to throw	threw	thrown
to understand	understood	understood
to wear	wore	worn
to win	won	won
to write	wrote	written